Mass.) American Tract Society (Boston

Lucy Raymond

The children's watchword

Mass.) American Tract Society (Boston

Lucy Raymond
The children's watchword

ISBN/EAN: 9783741166419

Manufactured in Europe, USA, Canada, Australia, Japa

Cover: Foto ©Andreas Hilbeck / pixelio.de

Manufactured and distributed by brebook publishing software (www.brebook.com)

Mass.) American Tract Society (Boston

Lucy Raymond

LUCY RAYMOND;

OR,

THE CHILDREN'S WATCHWORD.

BY A LADY OF ONTARIO.

AMERICAN TRACT SOCIETY,
150 NASSAU-STREET, NEW YORK.

Entered, according to Act of Congress, in the year 1871, by the AMERICAN TRACT SOCIETY, in the Office of the Librarian of Congress, at Washington.

Contents

I.	Miss Preston's Last Sunday .... PAGE	5
II.	Lucy's Home	22
III.	More Home Scenes	39
IV.	Nelly's Sunday Evening	55
V.	Strawberrying	67
VI.	A Mission	83
VII.	Temptations	99
VIII.	Partings	123
IX.	Introductions	146
X.	New Experiences	162
XI.	A Start in Life	182
XII.	Ambition	204
XIII.	A Friendship	226
XIV.	An Unexpected Recognition	245

XV.	The Flo	62
XVI.	Darknes	77
XVII.	Home A	97
XVIII.	A Farew	10

LUCY RAYMOND.

I.

MISS PRESTON'S LAST SUNDAY.

> "Tell me the old, old story
> Of unseen things above;
> Of Jesus and His glory,
> Of Jesus and His love."

THE light of a lovely Sabbath afternoon in June lay on the rich green woodlands, still bright with the vivid green of early summer, and sparkled on the broad river, tossed by the breeze into a thousand ripples, that swept past the village of Ashleigh. It would have been oppressively warm but for the breeze which was swaying the long branches of the pine-trees around the little church, which from its elevation on the higher ground looked down upon the straggling clusters of white houses nestling in their orchards and gardens that sloped away below. The same breeze, pleasantly laden with the mingled fragrance of the pines and of the newly-cut hay, fanned the faces of the children, who, in pretty little groups—the flickering shadows of the pines falling on their light, fluttering summer dresses —were approaching the church, the grave demeanor of a few of the elder ones showing that their thoughts were already occupied by the pleasant exercises of the Sunday-school.

Along a quiet, shady path also leading to the church, a young lady was slowly and thoughtfully walking, on whose countenance a slight shade of sadness apparently contended with happier thoughts. It was Mary Preston's last Sunday in her old home, previous to exchanging it for the new one to which she had been looking forward so long; and full as her heart was of thankfulness to God for the blessings he had bestowed, she could not take farewell of the Sunday-school in which she had taught for several years, without some regret and many misgivings. Where, indeed, is the earnest teacher, however faithful, who can lay down the self-imposed task without some such feelings? Has the *heart* been in the work? Have thought and earnestness entered into the weekly instruction? Has a Christian example given force to the precepts inculcated? Above all, has there been earnest, persevering prayer to the Lord of the harvest, in dependence on whom alone the joyful reaping-time can be expected?

Such were some of the questions which had been passing through Miss Preston's mind, and the smile with which she greeted her class as she took her place was a little shadowed by her self-condemning reflections — reflections which her fellow-teachers would have thought quite uncalled for in one who had been the most zealous and conscientious worker in that Sunday-school. But Mary Preston little thought of comparing herself with others. She knew that to whom "much is given, of him shall be much required;" and judging herself by this standard, she felt how little she had rendered to the Lord for his benefits to her. As her wistful glance strayed during the opening hymn to the faces of her scholars, she could not help wondering what influence the remembrance of what she had tried to teach them would exert on their future lives.

As her class had been much diminished by recent changes, and in view of her approaching departure the blanks had not been filled up, it consisted on this Sunday of only three girls, of ages varying from twelve to fourteen, but differing much in appearance, and still more widely in character and in the circumstances of their lives.

Close to Miss Preston, and watching every look of the teacher she loved and grieved at losing, sat Lucy Raymond, the minister's motherless daughter, a slight, delicate-looking girl, with dark hair and bright gray eyes, full of energy and thought, but possessing a good deal of self-will and love of approbation, dangerous elements of character unless modified and restrained by divine grace.

Next to her sat fair, plump, rosy-cheeked, curly-haired Bessie Ford, from the Mill-Bank

Farm—an amiable, kind-hearted little damsel, and a favorite with all her companions, but careless and thoughtless, with a want of steadiness and moral principle which made her teacher long to see the taking root of the good seed, whose development might supply what was lacking.

Very different from both seemed the third member of the class—a forlorn-looking child, who sat shyly apart from the others, shrinking from proximity with their neat, tasteful summer attire, as if she felt the contrast between her own dress and appearance and that of her school-fellows. Poor Nelly Connor's dingy straw hat and tattered cotton dress, as well as her pale, meagre face, with its bright hazel eyes gleaming from under the tangled brown hair, showed evident signs of poverty and neglect. She was a stranger there, having only recently come to Ashleigh, and had been found wandering about, a Sunday or two before, by Miss Preston, who had coaxed her into the Sunday-school, and had kept her in her own class until she should become a little more familiar with scenes so strange and new. Curiosity and wonder seemed at first to absorb all her faculties, and her senses seemed so evidently engrossed with the novelty of what she saw around her that her teacher could scarcely hope she took in any of the instruction which in the most simple words she tried to impress on her wandering mind. And so very ignorant was she of the most elementary truths of Christianity that Miss Preston scarcely dared to ask her the simplest question, for fear of drawing towards her the wondering gaze of her more favored class-mates, who, accustomed from infancy to hear of a Saviour's love and sacrifice for sin, could scarcely comprehend how any child,

> "Born in Christian lands
> And not a heathen or a Jew,"

could have grown up to nearly their own age ignorant of things which were familiar to them as household words.

Lucy and Bessie, in their happy ignorance and inexperience, little dreamed how many thousands in Christian cities full of stately churches, whose lofty spires seem to proclaim afar the Christianity of the inhabitants, grow up even to manhood and womanhood with as little knowledge of the glorious redemption provided to rescue them from their sin and degradation as if they were sunk in the thickest darkness of heathenism. Strange that congregations of professed followers of Christ, whose consciences will not let them refuse to contribute some small portion of their substance to convey the glad tidings of the gospel to distant lands, will yet, as they seek their comfortable churches, pass calmly by whole districts where so many of their fellow-countrymen are perishing for lack of that very gospel, without making one personal effort to save them! Will they not have to give an account for these things?

Nelly Connor's life had for the last two or three years been spent in one of the lowest districts of the city in which her father had fixed his abode after his emigration from the "old sod" to the New World. The horrors of that emigration she could still remember—the over-crowded steerage, where foul air bred the dreaded "ship-fever," and where the moans of the sick and dying weighed down the hearts of those whom the disease had spared. Her two little sisters had died during that dreadful voyage, and her mother, heart-broken and worn out with fatigue and watching, only lived to reach land and die in the nearest hospital. An elder brother, who was to have accompanied them, had by some accident lost his passage, and though he had, they supposed, followed them in the next ship that sailed, they never discovered any further trace of him. So, when Nelly's father had followed his wife to the grave in the poor coffin he had with difficulty provided for her, he and his daughter were all that remained of the family which had set out from their dear Irish home, hoping, in the strange land they sought, to lay the foundation of happier fortunes.

They led an uncomfortable, unsettled life for a year or two after that, exchanging one miserable lodging for another, rarely for the better. The father obtained an uncertain employment as a deck hand on a steamboat during the summer, subsisting as best he could on odd jobs during the winter, and too often drowning his sorrows and cares in the tempting but fatal cup. Poor Nelly, left without any care or teaching, soon forgot all she had ever learned, and running wild with the neglected children around her, became, as might have been expected, a little street Arab, full of shrewd, quick observation, and utter aversion from restraint of any kind.

Suddenly, to Nelly's consternation, her father brought home a second wife, a comrade's widow, with two or three young children. In the new household, Nelly was at once expected to take the place of nurse and general drudge, a part for which her habits of unrestrained freedom and idleness had thoroughly disqualified her; and the results were what might have been expected. There was a good deal of heedlessness and neglect on Nelly's part, and nearly constant scolding on that of her new mother. And as the latter was neither patient nor judicious, and was moreover unreasonable in what she demanded from the child, there was many a conflict ending in sharp blows, the physical pain of which was nothing in comparison with the sense of injury and oppression left on the child's mind.

But she had no redress; for her father being so much away from his home, had no opportunity of opposing, as he would probably have done, his wife's severe method of "managing" his motherless child.

Things were in this condition when Mrs. Connor, who had formerly belonged to Ashleigh, made up her mind to remove thither, in the expectation both of living more cheaply, and of being able, among her old acquaintances, to find more work to eke out her uncertain means of living. Her husband was now working on a steamboat which passed up and down the river on which Ashleigh was situated, so that he could not see his family as often as before. They were now settled in a small, rather a dilapidated tenement, with a potato patch and pig-sty; and Mrs. Connor, who was an energetic woman, had already succeeded in making her family almost independent of the earnings which Michael Connor too often spent in the public house. This being the case, she had no scruples in providing for her own children without much consideration for Nelly, so that the poor child was a forlorn-looking object, when Miss Preston had found her hovering wistfully about, attracted by the sight of the children streaming towards the church, and had induced her to come, for the first time in her life, into a Sunday-school.

And now, with these three girls before her, differing so much in circumstances and culture, it was no wonder that Miss Preston should feel it a matter for earnest consideration what parting words she should say, which, even if unappreciated at the time, might afterwards come back to their minds, associated with the remembrance of a teacher they had loved, to help them in the conflict between good and evil which must have its place in their future lives. But she felt she could not possibly do better, in bidding farewell to her young pupils, than to direct them to Him who would never leave nor forsake them, who was nearer, wiser, tenderer, than any earthly friend; who, if they would trust themselves to Him, would guide them into all truth and in his own way of peace.

She had brought them each, as a little parting remembrancer, a pretty gift-card, bearing on one side the illuminated motto, "LOOKING UNTO JESUS," a text the blessed influence of which she herself had long experimentally known. And in words so simple as for the most part to reach even little Nelly's comprehension, she spoke earnestly of the loving Saviour to whom they were to "look;"· of that wonderful life, which, opening in the lowly manger of Bethlehem, and growing quietly to maturity in the green valleys of Nazareth, reached its full development in those unparalleled three years of "going about doing good," healing, teaching, warning, rebuking, comforting; not disdaining to stop and bless the little children; and at last dying to atone for our sins.

She explained to them that, although withdrawn from our earthly sight, he was as really near to them now, as he had been to those Jewish children eighteen hundred years ago; that their lowest whisper could reach him; that if they would but ask him he would be their truest Friend, ever at their side to help them to do right and resist temptation, to comfort them in sorrow, and sweeten their joy. Her earnest tone and manner, even more than her words, impressed the children, and fixed even Nelly Connor's bright hazel eyes in a wondering gaze. It was very new and strange to her to hear about the mysterious, invisible Friend who was so loving and kind: the idea of a *friend* of any kind being novel to the lonely, motherless child, more accustomed to harsh, unsparing reproof, than to any other language. Miss Preston, glad to see at least that her interest was excited, was fain to leave the germs of truth to take root and develop in her mind, under the silent influence of the divine Husbandman.

"Now, my dear children," she said, in conclusion, "whenever you are tempted to be careless or unfaithful in duty, to think that *it does n't matter because no one will know*, remember that your *Saviour knows;* that whatever the duty before you may be, you have to do it 'as to the Lord and not unto men.' Whenever you are tempted to get tired of trying to do right and resist temptation, or when you may feel sad for your sinfulness and unworthiness, think of the text I am leaving you, 'LOOKING UNTO JESUS.' And if you really and earnestly *look* to him, you will always find help, and strength, and guidance, and comfort."

On the reverse side of the illuminated card she had brought for her class, was printed, in clear, distinct characters, the hymn,

> "I lay my sins on Jesus,
>   The spotless Lamb of God;
> He bears them all, and frees us
>   From the accursed load.
> I lay my wants on Jesus,
>   All fullness dwells in him;
> He heals all my diseases,
>   He doth my soul redeem."

As Nelly could not read, Miss Preston had her say these verses several times after her, and as she had a quick ear, and a facility for learning by heart, she could soon repeat them. That she could not understand them at present, her teacher knew, but she thought it something gained that the words at least should linger in her memory, till their meaning should dawn upon her heart. Then telling Nelly she must take care of her pretty card, and try to learn to read it for herself, she bade her class an affectionate farewell, trusting that the Friend of whom she had been teaching them would care for them when *she* could not.

"I'll learn the hymn, miss, and try to learn to read it, if anybody 'll teach me," said Nelly, her bright brown eyes sparkling through tears, for her warm Irish heart had been touched by the kind words and tones of her teacher, whom she expected never to see again.

Bessie Ford's sunshiny face also looked unusually sorrowful, and Lucy Raymond's trembling lip bespoke a deeper emotion, with difficulty repressed.

"I shall see *you* again, Lucy," Miss Preston said, with a smile, as she affectionately detained her a moment, for Lucy had been invited to be present at her teacher's marriage, at which her father was to officiate. Lucy and Bessie walked away together, the former with her first experience of a "*last time*" weighing on her mind and spirits; and Nelly Connor slowly stole away among the trees toward the spot she called her "home."

Bessie's momentary sadness quickly vanished, as she engaged in a brisk conversation with another girl about her own age, who was eager to gossip about Miss Preston's approaching marriage, where she was going, and what she was to wear. Lucy drew off from her companion as soon as Nancy Parker joined them, partly from a real desire of thinking quietly of her teacher's parting words, partly in proud disdain of Bessie's frivolity. "How *can* she go on so," she thought, "after what Miss Preston has been saying?" But she forgot that disdain is as far removed from the spirit of the loving and pitying Saviour, as even the frivolity she despised.

"Come, Lucy, do n't be so stiff," said Nancy, as they approached the shady gate of the white house where Mr. Raymond lived, "can't you tell us something about the wedding? You 're going, are n't you?"

Nancy's pert, familiar tones grated upon Lucy's ear with unusual harshness, and she replied, rather haughtily, that she knew scarcely anything about it.

"Oh, no doubt you think yourself very

grand," Nancy rejoined; "but I can find out all about it from my aunt, and no thanks to you. Come on, Bessie." Bessie somewhat ashamed of her companion, and instinctively conscious of Lucy's disapproval, stopped at the gate to exchange a good-by with her friend, who for the moment was not very cordial.

Thus Miss Preston and her class had separated, and future days alone could reveal what had become of the seed she had tried to sow.

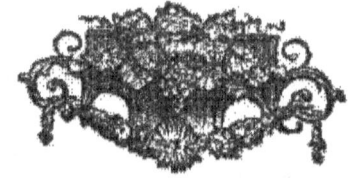

II.

LUCY'S HOME.

"Is the heart a living power?
  Self-entwined, its strength sinks low;
It can only live in loving,
  And by serving, love will grow."

AS Lucy passed in under the acacias which shaded the gate, she was met by a pretty, graceful-looking girl about her own age, who, with her golden hair floating on her shoulders and her hat swinging listlessly in her hand, was wandering through the shrubbery.

"Why, Lucy," she exclaimed, "what a time you have been away! I've tried everything I could think of, to pass the time; looked over all your books and could n't find a nice one I had n't read; teased Alick and Fred till they went off for peace, and pussy, till she scratched my arm—just look there!"

But Lucy's mind had been too much absorbed to descend at once to the level of her cousin's trifling tone, and having been vexed previously at her refusal to accompany her to Sunday-school, she now regretted exceedingly that Stella had not been present to hear Miss Preston's earnest words.

"O Stella," she said eagerly, "I do *so* wish you had been with me. If you had only heard what Miss Preston said to us, it would have done you good all your life."

"Well, you know I don't worship Miss Preston," replied Stella, always ready to tease; "she looks so demure. And as for dressing, why, Ada and Sophy wouldn't be seen out in the morning in that common-looking muslin she wore to church."

"O Stella, how can you go on so?" exclaimed Lucy, impatiently; "if you only had something better to think of you wouldn't talk as if you thought dress the one thing needful."

"That's a quotation from one of uncle Raymond's sermons, is n't it?" rejoined Stella aggravatingly.

Lucy drew her arm away from her cousin's, and walked off alone to the house, obliged to hear Stella's closing remark: "Well, I 'm glad *I* did n't go to Sunday-school, if it makes people come home cross and sulky!" And then, unconscious of the sting her words had implanted, Stella turned to meet little Harry, who was bounding home in his highest spirits.

Lucy slowly found her way to her own room, her especial sanctuary, where she had a good deal of pleasure in keeping her various possessions neatly arranged. At present it was shared by her young visitor, whose careless, disorderly ways were a considerable drawback to the pleasure so long anticipated, of having a companion of her own age. Just now her eye fell at once on her ransacked bookcase all in confusion, with the books scattered about the room. It was a trifle, but trifles are magnified when the temper is already discomposed, and throwing down her gloves and Bible, she hastily proceeded to rearrange them, feeling rather unamiably towards her cousin.

But as she turned back from the completed task, her card with its motto met her eye, like a gentle reproof to her ruffled spirit—"LOOKING UNTO JESUS." Had she not forgotten that already? She had come home enthusiastic; full of an ideal life she was to live, an example and influence for good to all around her. But mingled in her aspirations there was an unconscious desire for preëminence, and an insidious self-complacency, "little foxes," that will spoil the best grapes. She had to learn that God will not be served with unhallowed fire; that the heart must be freed from pride and self-seeking, before it can be fit for the service of the sanctuary. Already she knew she had been impatient and unconciliatory, contemptuous to poor ill-trained Nancy, whose home-influences were very unfavorable; and now, by her hastiness towards her cousin, whom she had been so anxious to influence for good, she had probably disgusted her with the things in which she most wanted to interest her.

She did not turn away, however, from the lights conscience brought to her. Nurtured in a happy Christian home, under the watchful eye of the loving father, whose care had to a great extent supplied the want of the mother she could scarcely remember, she could not have specified the time when she first began to look upon Christ as her Saviour, and to feel herself bound to live unto *Him* and not to herself. But her teacher's words had given her a new impulse—a more definite realization of the strength by which the Christian life was to be lived.

> "The mind to blend with outward life,
> While keeping at Thy side."

Humbled by her failure, she honestly confessed it and asked for more of the strength which every earnest seeker shall receive.

With a much lighter heart and clearer brow, Lucy went to rejoin Stella, whom she found amusing herself with Harry and his rabbits, having forgotten all about Lucy's hastiness. Lucy seated herself on the grass beside them, joining readily in the admiration with which Stella, no less than Harry, was caressing the soft, white, downy creature with pink eyes, which was her brother's latest acquisition.

"I want him to call it Blanche—such a pretty name, isn't it, Lucy?" said Stella.

"I wont," declared the perverse Harry, "because I don't like it;" and so saying he rushed off to join "the boys," as he called them.

"What have you got there?" asked Stella, holding out her hand for Lucy's card, which she had brought down. "Yes, it's pretty, but Sophy does much prettier ones; you should see some lovely ones she has done!"

"Has she?" asked Lucy with interest. "I think Stella's sister must care more for the Bible than she herself did, if she painted illuminated texts. I was going to tell you this was what Miss Preston was speaking to us about."

"I don't see that she could say much about that, it's so short; I don't see what it means; Jesus is in heaven now, and we can't see him."

"Oh, but," exclaimed Lucy eagerly, overcoming her shy reluctance to speak, "He is *always near*, though we can't see Him, and is ready to help us when we do right, and grieved and displeased when we do wrong. I forget that myself, Stella," she added with an effort, "or I shouldn't have been so cross when I came home."

Stella had already forgotten all about that, and felt a little uncomfortable at her cousin's entering on subjects which she had been accustomed to consider were to be confined to the pulpit, or at any rate were above her comprehension. She believed, of course, in a general way, that Christ had died for sinners, as she had often heard in church; and that in some vague way *she* was to be saved and taken to heaven, when she should be obliged to leave this world; but it had never occurred to her that the salvation of which she had been told was to influence her life *now*, or awaken any love from *her* in response to the great love which had been shown toward her. Not daring to reply, she glanced listlessly over the hymn on the card, but took up none of its meaning. She had never been conscious of any heavy burden of sin to be "laid on Jesus." Petted and praised at home for her beauty and lively winning ways, her faults overlooked and her good qualities exaggerated, she had no idea of the evil that lay undeveloped in her nature, shutting out from her heart the love of the meek and lowly Jesus. She could scarcely feel her need of strength for a warfare on which she had never entered; and Lucy's words, spoken out of the realizing experience she had already had, were to her incomprehensible.

She was a good deal relieved when the teabell rang and Lucy's two brothers, Fred and Harry, with her tall cousin Alick Steele, joined them as they obeyed the summons to the cool, pleasant dining-room, where Alick's mother, Mr. Raymond's sister, who had superintended his family since Mrs. Raymond's death, was already seated at the tea-table. Her quiet, gentle face, in the plain widow's cap, greeted them with a smile, brightening with a mother's pride and pleasure as she glanced towards her son Alick, just now spending a brief holiday at Ashleigh on the completion of his medical studies. He was a handsome, high-spirited youth, affectionate, candid, and full of energy, though as yet his mother grieved at his carelessness as to the "better part" which she longed to see him choose. He had always spent his vacations at Ashleigh, and was such a favorite that his visits were looked forward to as the pleasantest events of the year.

"Girls," said Alick, "I saw such quantities of strawberries this afternoon."

"Where?" interrupted Harry eagerly.

"Was anybody speaking to you?" asked his cousin, laughing. "But I'll tell you if you wont go and eat them all up. Over on the edge of the woods by Mill-Bank Farm. I could soon have filled a basket, if I had had one, and if mother wouldn't have said it was Sabbath-breaking!"

"Alick, my boy," said his mother gravely, "you mustn't talk so thoughtlessly; what would your uncle say?"

"He'd say it was a pity so good a mother hadn't a better son. But never mind, mother dear, you'll see I'll come all right yet. As for these strawberries, Lucy, I vote we have a strawberry picnic, and give Stella a taste of real country life. They'll give us cream at the farm, and the Fords would join us."

Stella looked a little of the surprise she felt at the idea of the farmer's children being added to the party, but she did not venture to say anything, as Alick was by no means sparing in bringing his powers of raillery to bear on what he called her "town airs and graces."

"Well, you needn't make all the arrangements to-night,' interposed Mrs. Steele; "you know your uncle does n't like Sunday planning of amusements."

And just then Mr. Raymond entered the room, his grave, quiet face, solemnized by the thoughts with which he had been engrossed, exercising an unconsciously subduing influence over the lively juniors. Mr. Raymond never frowned upon innocent joyousness, and even the boisterous little Harry was never afraid of his father; yet there was about him a certain realization of the great truths he preached, which checked any approach to levity in his presence, and impressed even the most thoughtless; although not tracing it to its real source, they generally set it down simply to his "being a clergyman." His children looked up to him with devoted affection and deep reverence;

even Stella could not help feeling that her uncle must be a *very* good man; and to Alick, who, under all his nonsense, had a strong appreciation of practical religion, he was the embodiment of Christian excellence.

"Well, Stella," said her uncle, turning kindly to his niece, "I hope you had a pleasant afternoon. I suppose our little Sunday-school looks very small after the great city ones."

"We never go to Sunday-school at home, uncle," said Stella, with one of her winning smiles. "There are so many *common* children."

"Oh, indeed!" exclaimed Alick, seizing the opportunity of putting down Stella's airs. "Why don't you get up a select one, then, attended only by young ladies of the best families?"

Stella colored at the sarcastic tone, but Mr. Raymond only said kindly, "Did you ever think, my dear child, how many of these poor common children, as you call them, you will have to meet in heaven?"

It was certainly a new idea to Stella, and made her feel rather uncomfortable; indeed, she never cared much to think about heaven, of which her ideas were the vaguest possible.

As they went to evening service, Alick did not omit to rally Stella on her want of candor in leaving her uncle under the impression that she had been at Sunday-school that afternoon.

"Why, Alick!" she exclaimed in surprise, "I didn't say I had been at Sunday-school. If uncle Raymond supposed so, it wasn't my fault."

"Only you answered him as if his supposition was correct; I have always understood that intentionally confirming a false impression was at least the next thing to telling a story."

"Well, I'm sure Stella didn't think of that," interposed Lucy, good-naturedly, noticing the rising color of vexation on Stella's countenance.

"How tiresome they all are here," thought Stella; "always finding out harm in things. I'm sure it wasn't my business to tell uncle William I hadn't been at Sunday-school. Sophy and Ada often tell the housemaid to say they are not at home, when they are, and don't think it any harm. What would Alick say to that?"

By one of those coincidences which sometimes happen—sent, we may be sure, in God's providence—Mr. Raymond took for his text, that evening the words, "Looking unto Jesus, the author and finisher of our faith." The coincidence startled Lucy and made her listen with more than ordinary attention to her father's sermon; though, to do her justice, she was not usually either sleepy or inattentive. Mr. Raymond began by alluding to the "race set before us," which the apostle had spoken of in the previous verse, the race which all who will follow Christ must know, but only in the strength He will supply. The young and strong might think themselves sufficient for it, but the stern experience of life would soon teach them that it must be often run with a heavy heart and weary feet; that "even the youths shall faint and be weary, and the young men utterly fall;" and that it is only they who wait on the Lord, "looking unto Jesus," who shall "mount up on wings as eagles," who shall "run and not be weary, and shall walk and not faint."

Then he spoke of the Helper ever near—

the "dear Jesus ever at our side," in looking to whom in faith and prayer, not trying to walk in our own strength, we may get

> "the daily strength
> To none who ask denied;"

the strength to overcome temptation and conquer sloth, and do whatever work he gives us to do. Something, too, he said of what that work is: First, the faithful discharge of daily duty, whatever its nature; then the more voluntary work for Christ and our fellow-men with which the corners of the busiest life may be filled up—the weak and weary to be helped, the mourner to be sympathized with, the erring brother or sister to be sought out and brought back, the cup of cold water to be given for Christ's sake, which should not lose its reward.

He ended by speaking of the grounds on which Jesus is the "author and finisher of our faith," the great salvation won by him for us on the cross, a salvation to be entered upon now, so that during this life we may begin that glorious eternal life which is to go on for ever. Then he besought his hearers, by the greatness of that love which had prompted the infinite sacrifice, by the endurance of that mysterious depth of suffering which the Son of God bore for men, that He might "save them to the uttermost that come unto God by Him," to come at once to have their sins washed away in the Redeemer's blood, which alone could "purge their consciences from dead works to serve the living God."

Many and many a time during Lucy's after-life did the words of that sermon come back to her mind, associated with her father's earnest, solemn tones, with the peaceful beauty of that summer Sabbath evening—with the old church, its high seats and pulpit and time-stained walls, and the old familiar faces whom all her life she had been wont to see, Sunday after Sunday, in the same familiar seats.

And what of the others? Bessie Ford, too, had noticed the coincidence, and had listened to the sermon as attentively as a somewhat volatile mind would allow her, and had gathered from it more than she could have put into conscious thought, though it was destined to bring forth fruit.

And far back, in a dusky corner of the little gallery, gleamed the bright brown eyes of little Nelly, who had ventured back to the church, and hearing the familiar sound of the text, listened intently and picked up some things which, though only half understood, yet awakened the chords which had been already touched to a trembling response.

Even little Harry in some measure abstained from indulging in his ordinary train of meditation during church-time, consisting chiefly of planning fishing excursions and games for the holidays. How many older and wiser heads are prone to the same kind of reverie, and could not have given a better account of "papa's sermon" than he was usually able to do? Fred, the quiet student, listened with kindling eye and deep enthusiasm to his father's earnest exposition of the divine truth which had already penetrated his own mind and heart; and Alick heard it with a reverent admiration for the beautiful gospel which could prompt such noble sentiments, and with a vague determination that "sometime" he would think about it in earnest.

Stella alone, of all the young group, carried away nothing of the precious truth which had been sounding in her ears. She had gone to church merely as a matter of form—without any expectation of receiving a blessing there; and during the service her wandering eyes had been employed in taking a mental inventory of the various odd and old-fashioned costumes that she saw around her, to serve for her sister's amusement when she should return home. It is thus that the evil one often takes away the good seed before it has sunk into our hearts. Stella would have been surprised, had it been suggested to her that the words of the last hymn, which rose sweetly through the church in the soft summer twilight, could possibly apply to her that evening:

> "If some poor wandering child of thine
> Have spurned to-day the voice divine,
> Now, Lord, the gracious work begin ;
> Let him no more lie down in sin !"

III.

MORE HOME SCENES.

"Tell me the story often,
For I forget so soon;
The early dew of morning
Has passed away at noon."

WHEN Bessie Ford parted from Lucy at the gate, she had still a long walk before reaching home. Mill-Bank Farm was a good mile and a half from the village if you went by the road, but Bessie shortened it very considerably by striking across the fields, a little way beyond the village. There were one or two fences to climb, but Bessie did not mind that any more than she minded the placid cows browsing in the pasture through which her way led. The breezy meadows, white with ox-eye daisies, and in some places yellow with buttercups, with the blue river flowing rapidly past on one side, afforded a pleasant walk at any time, and the rest of the way was still prettier. Just within the boundary of Mill-Bank Farm the ground ascended slightly, and then descended into a narrow glen or ravine, with steep, rocky sides luxuriantly draped with velvet moss and waving ferns, while along the bottom of it a little stream flowed quietly enough towards the river, though a little higher up it came foaming and dashing down the rocks and turned a small saw-mill on the farm. The sides of the ravine were shady with hemlocks, spreading their long, waving boughs over the rocks, with whose dark, solemn foliage maples and birches contrasted their fresh vivid green. In spring, what a place it was for wild flowers—as Lucy Raymond and her brothers well knew, having often brought home thence great bunches of dielytras and convallarias and orchises; and at any time some bright blossoms were generally to be found gleaming through the shade.

Bessie, however, did not linger now to look for them, but picking her way across the stepping-stones which lay in the bed of the stream, she quickly climbed the opposite bank by a natural pathway which wound up among the rocks—easily found by her accustomed feet—and passing through the piece of woodland that lay on the other side, came out on the sunny expanse of meadows and cornfields, in the midst of which stood the neat white farmhouse, with its little array of farm buildings, and the fine old butternut-tree, under the shade of which Mrs. Ford sat milking her sleek, gentle cows, little Jenny and Jack sitting on the ground beside her. The instant that they espied their sister coming through the fields, they dashed off at the top of their speed to see who should reach her first, and were soon trotting along by her side, confiding to her their afternoon's adventures, and how Jack had found nine eggs in an unsuspected nest in the barn, but had broken three in carrying them in.

"But me would n't have," insisted Jack, sturdily, "if Jenny had n't knocked up against me."

"O Jack! Now you know I only touched

you the least little bit," retorted the aggrieved Jenny.

"Well, don't jump up and down so, or I will let go your hand," said Bessie. "You almost pull my arm off! I wish you could see how quietly little Mary Thompson sits in Sunday-school, and she is no bigger than you."

"Why can't I go to Sunday-school then?" demanded Jenny; "I'd be quiet too!"

"And me too!" vociferated Jack; the circumstance that they were not considered old enough yet to go to Sunday-school giving it a wonderful charm in their eyes. Then, as they set off again on another race toward their mother, it occurred to Bessie for the first time that these little ones were quite old enough to learn the things that other little children learned at Sunday-school, and that although they were not strong enough for the long walk, and her mother's time and thoughts were always so fully engrossed with the round of domestic duties, *she* might easily find time to teach her little brother and sister as much as they could understand about the Saviour, who had died that they might be made good; and who when on earth had blessed little children. Something Miss Preston had said about home duties—about helping to teach and guide the little brothers and sisters—now recurred to her mind, and conscience told her that these duties she had hitherto failed of performing. She had never herself really taken Christ for her own Saviour and Guide, although she often felt a vague wish that she were "good," and the desire of pleasing Christ entered but little, if at all, into the motives and actions of her daily life. But she generally *knew* what was right, and occasionally, while the impulse from some good influence was still fresh, would try to *do* it.

"I know Miss Preston would say I ought to teach Jenny and Jack some verses and hymns on Sunday," she thought. "I'll begin to-night, when mother and the boys are gone to church;" for a certain shyness about seeming "good" made her wish to begin her teaching without witnesses.

"Here, Bessie," said Mrs. Ford as Bessie approached, "do run and get the tea ready, there's a good girl. I sha'n't be through yet for half an hour, for I've the calves to see to and your father and the boys'll be in from watering the horses, and if we don't get tea soon they'll be late for church."

Bessie went in to change her dress, with her usually good-humored face contracted into a dissatisfied expression. She was tired; it would have been nice to sit down and read her Sunday-school book till tea-time. But of course nothing could be said, so she hurriedly pulled off her walking things, grumbling a little in her own mind at the difference between her own lot and that of Lucy Raymond, who, she felt sure, had none of these tiresome things to do. She had never thought—what, indeed, older people often lose sight of—that God so arranges the work of all his children who will do what he gives them to do, that while some may seem to have more leisure than others, all have their appointed work, of the kind best suited to discipline and fit them for the higher sphere of nobler work, in which will probably be found much of the blessedness of eternity.

Before Bessie went down to her unwelcome task, she recollected that she must put her pretty card safe out of the children's way; so with a strong pin she fastened it up securely on the wall, to which it formed a tasteful decoration. As she did so, the motto brought back to her memory what Miss Preston had said about "looking unto Jesus" in every time of temptation, great or small, as well when inclined to be discontented or impatient, as in greater emergencies. The evil principle in her nature rose against her doing so now, but the other power was stronger, and perhaps for the first time in her life, though she regularly "said her prayers," Bessie really asked Jesus to help her to be more like himself. Then with a new, strange happiness in her heart, that was at once the result of her self-conquest and the answer to her prayer, she ran down cheerfully to do her work, singing in a low tone the first verse of her hymn:

> "I long to be like Jesus,
> Meek, loving, lowly, mild,
> I long to be like Jesus,
> The Father's holy child."

Jenny and Jack came running in to help her; small assistants whom it required a good deal of patience to manage, neither allowing them to hurt themselves or anything else, nor driving them into a fit of screaming by despotically thwarting their good intentions; and Bessie's patience was not always equal to the ordeal. But on this occasion, Mrs. Ford was left to pursue her dairy avocations in peace, without being called in by Jack's screams to settle some fierce dispute between him and his sister, whose interference was not always very judiciously applied.

The tea was soon ready, not, however, before Mr. Ford and his two eldest boys had come in, accompanied by Bessie's younger brother Sam, next in age to herself, who ought to have been at Sunday-school, but had managed to escape going, as he often did. His mother being on Sundays as on other days, "cumbered with much serving," and his sister generally remaining with some of her friends in the village during the interval between the morning service and Sunday-school, it was comparatively easy for Master Sam to play truant, as indeed he sometimes did from the day-school, where his chances of punishment were much greater. Mr. Ford being far more alive to the advantages of a "good education" than to the need of the knowledge which "maketh wise unto salvation." So that when Bessie began her usual "Why, Sam, you were n't at Sunday-school!" Sam had some plausible excuse all ready, the ingenuity of which would amuse his father so much as to lead him to overlook the offence.

"Well, Bessie," her mother exclaimed, when they were all seated, "I really believe you have n't forgotten anything, for *once!* I should not wonder if you were to turn out a decent housekeeper yet."

For it was Mrs. Ford's great complaint of Bessie that she was so "heedless" and "needed so much minding," though she would always add, modifying her censure, "but then, you can't put an old head on young shoulders; and the child has a real good *heart*." And being a thoroughly active and diligent housekeeper, she generally found it less trouble to supply Bessie's shortcomings herself, so that Bessie's home education was likely to suffer by her mother's very proficiency, unless she should come to see that to do all things well was a duty she owed "unto the Lord, and not unto men."

"So, Bessie, you're going to lose your teacher," said her father. "I hear she's to be married on Thursday."

"Yes, father, she bade us all good-by to-day, and she gave us such pretty cards, mother, with a text and a hymn;" and on the impulse of the moment she ran up for hers, and brought it down for inspection. It was handed round the table, eliciting various admiring comments, and exciting Jack's desire to get it into his own hands, which being thwarted, he was with difficulty consoled by an extra supply of bread and butter.

"And, mother," asked Bessie, somewhat doubtfully, "may I go to-morrow and get the things to work a book-mark for Miss Preston? I'd like to do it for a new Bible the teachers are going to give her."

"I don't care," said Mrs. Ford, "if you'll only not neglect everything else while you're doing it. I don't believe in girls fiddling away their time with such things, and not knowing how to make good cheese and butter. But I would n't hinder you from making a present to Miss Preston, for she has been a good teacher to you."

Bessie looked delighted, but the expression quickly changed when her mother said, as they rose from table, "Bessie, I guess I'll not go to church to-night. I've had so much to do that I feel tired out; and if I did go, I'm sure I'd just go to sleep. Besides, I don't like the way the dun cow is looking; so you'd better get ready and go with father and the boys."

Now Bessie had expected to remain at home that evening, as she usually did. She had planned to teach the children for awhile, according to her new resolution, and then when they had gone to bed, to sit down to read her Sunday-school book, which seemed unusually inviting. Bessie's Sunday reading was generally confined to her Sunday-school book, for she had not yet learned to love to read the Bible, and regarded it rather as a lesson-book, than as the spiritual food which those who know it truly find "sweeter than honey" to their taste. So it was not a very pleasant prospect to have to hurry off to church again, and she felt very much inclined to make the most of the slight fatigue she felt, and say she was too tired to go, in which case her mother would have willingly assented to her remaining. But conscience told her she was able to go, and ought to go; and remembering her motto and her prayer, she cheerfully prepared to accompany her father and brothers to church, and she had reason to be grateful for her choice. The words of the sermon deepened and expanded the impressions of the afternoon, and left an abiding influence on the current of her life.

When Mrs. Ford had got through her evening duties, and the little ones were hushed in sound slumber, she sat down near the open window to rest, her eye falling, as she did so, on Bessie's card. The motto upon it carried her thoughts away to the time when, as a newly-married wife, she had listened to a sermon on that very text; a time when, rejoicing in the happiness of her new life, she had felt her heart beat with gratitude to Him who had so freely given her all things, and with a sincere desire to live to His glory. How had the desire been carried out? A very busy life hers had been, and still was. The innumerable cares and duties of her family, and farm, and dairy, had filled it with never-ceasing active occupations, as was natural and right; but was it right that these occupations should have so crowded out the very principle that would have given a holy harmony to her life, and been a fountain of strength to meet the cares and worries that will fret the stream of the most prosperous course. Sacred words, learned in her childhood, recurred to her mind: "And the cares of this world, and the deceitfulness of riches, and the lusts of other things, entering in, choke the word, and it becometh unfruitful." Had not that been her own experience? Where were the fruits that might have been expected from "the word" in her? the Christian influence and training which might have made her household what a Christian household ought to be?

Had not the "cares of this world" been made the chief concern; the physical and material well-being of her family made far more prominent than the development of a life hid with Christ in God? Had not the very smoothness and prosperity of her life, and her self-complacency in her own good management, been a snare to her? Her husband—good and kind as he was—was, she knew, wholly engrossed with the things of this life; and her boys—steadier, she often thought with pride, than half the boys of the neighborhood—had never yet been made to feel that they were not their own, but bought with the price of a Saviour's blood. Such higher knowledge as Bessie had was due to Miss Preston, for like many mother, she had not scrupled to devolve her own responsibilities on the Sunday-school teachers, and thought her duty done when she had seen her children neatly dressed set off to school on Sunday afternoon. And the little ones she had just left asleep—had she earnestly commended them to the Lord, and tried to teach them such simple truths about their Saviour, as their infant minds could receive?

All these thoughts came crowding into her

mind, as they sometimes will, when the voice of the Spirit can find an entrance into our usually closed hearts; and she shrank from the thought of the account she should have to give of the responsibilities abused, the trust unfulfilled. Happily, she did not forget that "if we confess our sins, He is faithful and just to forgive us our sins;" and that quiet hour of meditation and confession, and humble resolve, was one of the most profitable seasons Mrs. Ford had ever known. For God, unlike man, can work without as well as with outward instrumentality.

When the others returned from church, it was with some surprise that Mrs. Ford heard from Bessie the words of the text.

"I heard Mr. Raymond preach from that same text long ago, just after we were married, John," she said.

"Well, if you remember it, it's more than I do; but if he did preach the same sermon over again, it is well worth hearing twice."

"Yes, indeed," said his wife. "I wish I had minded it better. It would have been better for us all if we had. Bessie, are you too tired to read a chapter as soon as the boys come in? We don't any of us read the Bible enough, I'm afraid."

And Bessie, struck by something unusual in her mother's tone and manner, cheerfully read aloud, at Mrs. Ford's request, the thirteenth of Matthew and the tenth of Hebrews, although the tempting Sunday-school book still lay unread on the table up stairs.

IV.

NELLY'S SUNDAY EVENING.

"Oh, say not, dream not—heavenly notes
   To childish ears are vain ;
That the young mind at random floats,
   And cannot catch the strain."

IN the meantime, let us go back to Nelly Connor, and see how *she* spent her Sunday afternoon.

When she had wistfully watched the last of the groups of children disappearing in the distance, she walked slowly away toward her "home"—a dilapidated-looking cottage, in a potato-patch, enclosed by a broken-down fence, patched up by Nelly and her new mother with old barrel-staves and branches of trees. The out-door work which fell to her lot Nelly did not so much dislike. It was the nursing a screaming baby, or scrubbing dingy, broken boards—work often imposed upon her—which sorely tried her childish strength and patience.

Nelly found the house deserted. Sunday being Mrs. Connor's idle day, she usually went to visit some of her friends in the village, taking her children with her. A piece of bread and a mug of sour milk on the table were all that betokened any preparation for Nelly's supper, but she was glad enough to miss the harsh, scolding tones that were her usual welcome home.

Nelly sat down on the doorstep to eat her crust, watching, as she did so, a little bird which was bringing their evening meal to its chirping little ones in a straggling old plum-tree near the house. For in animal life there is no such discord as sin introduces into human life, marring the beauty of God's arrangements for his creatures' happiness. Then, having nothing to keep her at home, she took up her dingy, tattered straw hat and strolled slowly along towards the village, keeping to the shady lanes on its outskirts till she came out upon the fields across which Bessie had taken her way home.

On her way she passed Mr. Raymond's pretty shrubbery, and stood for a while quite still by the white railings, looking at the group within: Lucy and her cousin sitting under the trees on the green turf, with Harry and the rabbit close beside them. Nelly thought she had never seen anything so pretty as Stella, with her rose-leaf complexion and sunny golden hair. The two might have served a painter for a contrast, both as to externals and as to the effect of the surrounding influences which mould human life: the one, from her cradle so tenderly and luxuriously nurtured, petted, and caressed; the other, accustomed from her earliest years to privation and hardship, to harsh tones and wicked words, to all the evil influences which surround a child left to pick up its education on the city streets. Strange mystery of the "election of circumstances!"—one of the strangest in our mystery-surrounded life, never to be cleared up till all crooked things shall be made straight. Only let the privileged ones, whose lines have fallen in pleasant places, remember that "to whom much is given, of them much shall be required."

A forlorn little figure Nelly looked as she strolled along the field-paths which Bessie had taken an hour before. But she did not trouble herself much about externals, except when brought in company with others whose better attire made her painfully conscious of the defects in her own; and being of a nature open to every impression from surrounding objects, she was at that moment far from being an unhappy child. It was not often that she was completely free to wander at will, and the fresh breezy fields, the sweet scents of the clover and the pines, the blue, rippling river, and the cows that looked calmly at her with their patient, wistful eyes, were all novelties to the town child, whose first summer it was in the country. Some faint recollections she still had of the grassy slopes of her native hills, in the days of her early childhood; but since then, all her experiences of summer had been the hot, hard pavements and stifling dust of a large city.

She had never before extended her wanderings in the direction of Mill-Bank Farm so far as to reach the ravine through which the little stream flowed into the river; and now when she came to the edge of the steep slope and looked down into the luxuriant depth of foliage and fern and ragged moss-clad rock, she felt a sense of delight more intense than Bessie Ford or Lucy Raymond, familiar all their lives with such scenes, had ever experienced. She stood spell-bound at first, and then, scrambling down among rock and fern, reached the little stream, and was soon wading about in its bed, enjoying the sensation of the soft, warm water flowing over her bare feet, and pulling the little flowering water-plants that raised their heads among the moss-grown logs and stones which lay in the bed of the stream. Then she began to climb up on the other side, stopping to examine with admiring eyes every velvety cushion of moss, and cluster of tiny ferns, and fairy-like baby pine or maple, and picking with eager hands the wild roses and other blossoms which she espied among the tangled underwood.

At last, tired with her wanderings, and with hands full of her treasures, she threw herself down on a bed of dry moss that carpeted the top of a high bank of rock which overlooked the river winding away beneath, while overhead, through the feathery sprays of the long, straggling pine boughs, the slanting sunbeams flickered on the turf below.

There, in that solitary stillness—all the stiller for the confused murmur of soft sounds, and the fresh, sweet breath of the woods perfuming the air—unaccustomed thoughts came into the little girl's mind; thoughts which in the din and bustle of the city, where the tide of human interests sufficed to fill up her undeveloped mind, had scarcely ever entered it. But here, where the direct works of God alone were around her, her mind was irresistibly drawn towards Him of whom Miss Preston had told her that He had made her and all she saw around her, and who lived, she supposed, somewhere beyond that blue sky. With so many pleasant things around her, the thought of their Maker was pleasant too. But then, Miss Preston had told her that God loved what was good, but hated what was bad; and did not her new mother constantly tell her she was a "bad child," an accusation in which her conscience told her there was much truth? So God could not love her, she thought.

But Miss Preston had said that God did love her; that he cared for her continually, and wished to make her good and happy; that he had even, in some strange way which she could not understand, sent his Son to die for her, that she might be made good. It was all new and strange, but she had faith in Miss Preston, and because she had told her she believed it must be true that she, who had come to think herself—poor child—too bad for any one to care for, had really a great, kind Friend, near her though she could not see him, and loving her more than the mother whose warm caress she could still remember. It was an idea that might seem beyond the grasp of a poor untaught child, were it not that He who reveals himself to babes and sucklings can speak to the heart he has made in ways beyond our power to trace. The idea in Nelly's mind of that wonderful love which she so sorely needed, was more enlightened than many a philosopher's conception of Divinity, and the dark eyes filled with tears as a half-formed prayer awoke from her heart to the loving Jesus, who, Miss Preston had told her, would hear and answer her.

And who could doubt that He did hear and answer the desolate, uncared-for child, scarcely knowing as yet what "good" meant, since her knowledge had been only of evil! Her conscience, however, was not dead, though neglected; she knew at least what "wrong" was, and felt she must leave off doing it, if the Saviour was to be her friend. But how should she be able to leave off her bad, idle ways and become a good, industrious girl, such as her new mother said most of the little girls in Ashleigh were? Then she remembered the words which Miss Preston had made her repeat: "Looking unto Jesus," and "I lay my sins on Jesus;" and that Miss Preston had told her she must ask Jesus to take away her sins and make her good. But she thought the right place for speaking to Jesus must be in the church, as most of the people she had known in the city used to go to church to "confess," and she supposed that must have something to do with it.

Just then she saw the Fords passing at a little distance, on their way to church, and it occurred to her that she would go too, and perhaps Jesus would hear her there and show her how she was to be made good. So she started up, and was speedily on the other side of the ravine, almost overtaking the Fords before they reached the village. The service was beginning when she crept stealthily into one of the farthest back seats, half afraid lest she was doing wrong in thus trespassing where she had no right. Then crouched in a corner, with her face bent forward and her elf-locks half covering her eyes, she listened with intense earnestness, trying to take in all she could of what was so new, yet already not unfamiliar to her, and half disposed to think that the kindly-looking gentleman who stood there and spoke in such solemn tones might be Jesus himself.

Let not the more favored ones, on whom from their cradles the blessed light of Divine truth has steadily shone, smile at this poor child's ignorance, but, rather, try to show their gratitude for higher privileges by seeking to impart some of the light shed on them so abundantly to those who are still wandering in darkness.

On Nelly's listening heart Mr. Raymond's sermon did not fall so fruitlessly as some might have expected. For God is, for all, the hearer and answerer of prayer, and he never leaves unheard the weakest cry to him. As the lonely child once more sought her comfortless home, she felt a stirring of new hope within her, and scarcely minded her mother's rough words, when she demanded, "What have you been doing out so late? No good, I am sure!"

Mrs. Connor had been enlarging, among sympathizing friends, on the hardship of her having to support her husband's child, when he did so little himself for his family. "My goodness! all he gives us wouldn't half pay Nelly's board," she had declared; and as her grievances were still fresh in her mind, she greeted her stepchild with even more asperity than usual.

But as Nelly crept away to her hard little bed, perhaps some angel, sent to minister to the motherless child, may have known that the "good-for-nothing," ignorant little girl, oppressed with the feeling of her own sinfulness and full of the thought of her new-found heavenly Friend, was nearer the kingdom of heaven than the petted, admired, winning Stella Brooke, who had never yet learned her need of the Saviour, who came "not to call the righteous, but sinners, to repentance."

V.

STRAWBERRYING.

"Why should we fear youth's draught of joy,
If pure, would sparkle less?
Why should the cup the sooner cloy
Which God has deigned to bless?"

THE "strawberry picnic" proposed by Alick Steele had been fixed for the following Tuesday, should it prove fine. Alick and Fred had been over at Mill-Bank Farm, and the younger Fords had agreed to meet them at the ravine, with their contribution of milk and cream, and various other things which Mrs. Ford's zealous housewifery would not be prevented from sending, though Fred assured her that it was unnecessary.

"I know what young folks can eat, Mr. Fred," she replied, "and you may as well have plenty;" and Alick laughingly assured her she was quite right. Alick Steele, or the "young doctor," as his old friends now began to call him, had been an acceptable guest at many a picnic and merry-making, but he had never entered into anything of the kind with more spirit and zeal, than he now threw into this simple gypsying excursion with his country cousins.

"He's no end of a fellow for a picnic," declared Harry enthusiastically, "and ten times as good as Fred;" the quiet nature of the latter always shrinking from any unusual bustle, while Alick's unfailing flow of animal spirits found a congenial outlet in any little extra-excitement, especially when it was connected with the procuring of enjoyment for others. He and Harry were busy all Monday in exploring the ground and selecting the most eligible place for the repast, and Harry averred, when they returned home, that they would have "a splendid time" next day, if it were only fine.

Next morning opened as fair and bright as the excursionists could desire; not too hot, but tempered by a pleasant breeze—"just the day for the woods and not too rough for the water." For Stella had manifested such consternation at the idea of going through the pasture—"cows always frightened her so"—that notwithstanding the raillery and the representations of Alick and Harry, it was evident that her pleasure would be spoiled if she were obliged to go by the field-path. Alick, therefore, had good-naturedly hunted up a boat, which would save them a long, dusty walk by the road, and greatly enhance the pleasure of the excursion, besides carrying the "*impedimenta*," as Fred classically termed the baskets of provisions. Marian Wood, a playmate of Lucy's, was to accompany them in the boat, while Mrs. Steele and the boys walked across the fields.

As soon as the early dinner could be got over, the boat's cargo was taken on board, the passengers embarked, and after some little screams from Stella, who had a habit of being "nervous," the little bark shot off, swift and straight, impelled by Alick's firm, skilful strokes. The water-party reached the mouth of the

ravine considerably sooner than the others. and while awaiting their arrival, Alick rowed them to a little fairy islet near the shore, where they landed to explore it, and twine their hats with the graceful creepers and ferns growing among its rocks. Then reëmbarking, they floated at leisure up and down the glassy shaded water fringed with tall reeds, the girls alternately trying their hands at the oars, till a shout from Harry and the waving of handkerchiefs announced the arrival of the rest of the party.

The strawberry-pickers had soon begun their search. Fred, who preferred rowing to strawberry-picking, undertook to take charge of Harry, who was as eager for the water as a young duck, while Mrs. Steele taking out her knitting, sat down beside the baskets under a spreading oak, on a knoll overlooking the river, to wait until there should be a demand for tea.

Very quickly the time sped away, while the children pursued their busy but not laborious quest of the tempting berries—half hidden under their spreading leaves—and many an exclamation, half of annoyance, half of amusement, was uttered, as one of them made a dart at a bright spot of crimson, fancying it a rich cluster of berries, and finding only a leaf.

"Why in the world do strawberries have red leaves, I wonder!" exclaimed Harry, who, tired at last of boating, was pretending to help them, though they all declared he ate as many as he picked.

"To inure you to the disappointments of life," responded Alick oracularly. "You'll find, as you go along, there are more red strawberry-leaves than berries, all through."

And Alick half sighed, as if he had already learned the lesson by experience.

"There's one thing, Alick, of which that remark doesn't hold good," remarked Fred to his cousin, in an under tone. "My father says *that* sheet-anchor will bear us up through all the disappointments of life. And I believe it."

"Well, very likely you're right; well for those who can feel it so. But at present 1 can't say I belong to that happy number. Some time or other, perhaps; you know my head has been full of all sorts of ologies, except theology, for a good while back."

"The 'more convenient season,' Alick," replied Fred, with a half smile.

"Here, a truce to moralizing; who's got the most strawberries? The premium is to be the finest bunch in the collection," shouted Alick.

And after the prize had been with much ceremony and mirth adjudged to Bessie Ford, it was time to think about tea.

"Come," said Alick, "shoulder arms—that is, baskets, and march!"

All were very ready to obey Alick's word of command, and the merry party were soon collected around the snowy table-cloth spread on the turf, on which Mrs. Steele had arranged the tempting repast of pies and cakes, curds and cream, to which a fine large dish of strawberries—a contribution from the farm—formed a tempting addition.

Fred, at his aunt's request, asked a blessing, and then the good things were welcomed by the appetites sharpened by fresh air and exercise, and the feast was enlivened by the innocent glee and frolic which usually enliven such simple country parties, unfettered by form, and unsophisticated by any of the complications which creep into more elaborate picnics. Even Stella, though she felt the whole affair—especially the presence of the farmer's children—rather below her dignity as an embryo city belle, gave herself up unrestrainedly to the enjoyment of the occasion, and was more natural and free from what Alick called "airs," than she had been at any time during her visit. But the party were quite unconscious that they were watched, through the thickly drooping boughs of a large hickory, by a pair of bright, dark eyes, which were wistfully regarding them. The eyes were those of Nelly Connor, who, having been unexpectedly left free that afternoon to follow her own devices, had wandered away in the direction of the spot which had so fascinated her on Sunday.

When the tea was fairly over, and cups, dishes, and other paraphernalia were being packed up by Mrs. Steele and the girls, Stella, who, not being inclined to assist in such a menial occupation, was wandering aimlessly about, made a discovery.

"O Lucy," she exclaimed, coming hurriedly up to her, "there is such a ragged, bold-looking little girl sitting over there! She has been watching us the whole time."

"Well, her watching wouldn't hurt us," said Lucy, smiling at her cousin's consternation. "I hope she was pleased with what she saw. Why, it's Nelly Connor," she added, as the little girl emerged from her hiding-place. "What can have brought *her* here? I'll get aunt Mary to give her something to eat. I dare say she's hungry enough, for Miss Preston told me she didn't think her new mother gave her enough to eat."

"I think she ought to be scolded and sent away," said Stella decidedly. "You are just encouraging her impertinence in coming here to watch us."

But Lucy had already run off to her aunt, and was soon carrying a plate heaped with good things to the astonished Nelly, who, frightened at being discovered, and at Stella's frowning looks, was thinking how she might make good her escape. Stella had only spoken as she had been accustomed to hear those around her speak. She had been brought up to look upon poverty and rags as something almost wicked in themselves, and had never realized that feelings the same as her own might lie under an exterior she despised. She had never been taught the meaning of, "I was a hungered and ye gave me meat; I was thirsty and ye gave me drink." Lucy, on the contrary, had been taught to consider it the highest privilege and gratification to impart a share of the bounties bestowed upon herself to the poor and needy whom our Saviour has left as a legacy to his followers, and had already tasted the happiness of lightening somewhat the load of poverty and hardship which press upon some during all their lives.

She soon reassured Nelly, and had the satisfaction of seeing her enjoy the food with the zest of one to whom such delicacies were rare indeed, and whose appetite was very seldom fully satisfied at home. She explained to the rest that Nelly was in her class at Sunday-school, and Stella mentally put it down as another objection to going there, that it involved the possibility of such undesirable acquaintanceships. Alick was much interested in the little wanderer, and even after the rest had set off towards the farmhouse, which they were to visit before returning, he remained beside her, drawing from her, bit by bit, her touching history, until she began to remember how late it was, and started homeward, much astonished and cheered by the kindness and sympathy she had met with.

Alick found the rest of the party exploring the farmyard, admiring the cows, particularly Mrs. Ford's sleek, glossy black favorite, while Harry was, to his intense delight, cantering up and down the road to the gate, on the stout little pony which the farmer usually rode to market.

As there was a full moon, there was no hurry about returning, and on the arrival of Mr. Raymond, who had walked over to meet them, Mrs. Ford insisted on their coming in for awhile. And before they took their leave, she brought out her large family Bible for evening worship, with the request that Mr.

Raymond would read and pray before his departure; "for," she said, "I know we don't mind these things half enough, and we'd be all the better of a word or two from you."

Mr. Raymond read the last chapter of Ecclesiastes, making a few brief but impressive comments on the insufficiency for true happiness of the enjoyments which this life can furnish, fair and good gifts of God though such enjoyments may be. "The time would come, even in this life," he said, "when the joys of this world would be found wanting; and after this life, what would be their condition who had made this world their portion, and had 'not remembered their Creator in the days of their youth'?" Doubtless the thought of his own youthful circle, and of the strong, ruddy young Fords, all so full of health, and life, and joyous spirits, was strongly upon him when he dwelt so earnestly upon the words: "Rejoice, O young man, in thy youth, and let thy heart cheer thee in the days of thy youth, and walk in the ways of thy heart, and in the sight of thine eyes; but know thou, that for all these things God will bring thee into judgment."

Then, reading part of the third chapter of the first Epistle of John, he directed his hearers to the wonderful privileges provided for them, so far transcending all mere temporal gifts; to the "love the Father hath bestowed, that we should be called the sons of God;" showing how these privileges were to be grasped through faith in the love which laid down life for us; and how that love, flowing into the heart, was to purify the life by enabling us to do the things which are pleasing in His sight.

The solemn, earnest words—few, but well chosen—seeming to come with peculiar power after the day of joyous excitement, touched responsive chords in the hearts of most of the young party, who looked earnest and thoughtful; though who could tell whether the impression should be an abiding one, or should pass away like the "early dew"? Lucy and Bessie listened with real interest; the latter, especially, with much more than she would have felt a few days before; and Mrs. Ford silently renewed her good resolutions to seek to influence her family to choose the " better part, which could not be taken away from them."

Lucy could not help glancing at Stella when the verses in the chapter about want of compassion for the brother or sister in need were read; but Stella looked placidly unconscious, and, indeed, her thoughts were far away, considering how she should best impress Marian Wood, on their way home, with a due sense of the grandeur of her city life.

After many kind parting salutations and warm invitations from Mrs. Ford to come soon and spend an afternoon at the farm, the party took leave; one division proceeding homeward by the winding road, lying white in the full moonlight, as the fields were now wet with dew; while the others took the shortest cut to the river, where the boat was lying. Very little was said during most of the way, except some subdued exclamations of delight as they passed out from the deep shadow of the overhanging rocks into the broad river, which glittered in the moonlight like a sheet of dazzling silver, roughened by the slightest ripple, and past point after point of luxuriant foliage,

STRAWBERRYING.

looking dream-like and unreal in the light that silvered their glistening leaves.

As they neared the village, Lucy suddenly recollected their unexpected guest. "I wonder how Nelly got home; did she stay long after we left, Alick?" she said.

"No; she said her mother would be angry if she were out late, so she set off at a run."

"Lucy," said Stella, "I wonder how you can have anything to do with such a vagabond-looking child; I'm sure she was watching to see whether she could pick up anything; and she looked just like a gypsy!"

"O Stella! how can you be so suspicious?" exclaimed Lucy indignantly. "I don't believe Nelly would do any such thing! No wonder the poor child was watching us while we were at tea; didn't you see how hungry she was?"

"Well, I know we've had things stolen by just such children, and papa says it's best to keep such people down, for they're sure to impose on those who are kind to them, and charity is quite thrown away upon them."

"A convenient belief to save trouble," Lucy

was just going to say, but wisely repressed the impulse, feeling that it would not sound very respectful to Stella's father, who, she felt, must be a very different man from her own.

"Stella," said Alick, "did it ever occur to you what *you* might have been, if you had been left, motherless and almost fatherless, to run all day on the streets, listening to bad words and seeing all sorts of evil, without any one to say a kind word to you and teach you what is right? I wish you could have heard the poor little thing's story, as she told it to me." And in a few words he gave them an outline of Nelly's history.

"Papa says you never can believe their stories," objected the city-hardened Stella.

"I know you can't always," replied Alick, "but I think I'm not easily taken in, and I'm willing to stake my judgment on this being no sham! And how would *you* have turned out from such a bringing-up, Mademoiselle Stella?"

"And where is her father?" Lucy asked.

"Oh, her father works on a boat and is seldom at home. They came to live here because it is cheaper, and they can have a pig, and raise potatoes."

"I wonder whether she can read," said Lucy.

"I shouldn't think so, for she never was at school in her life; nor at church either, since they left Ireland, till last Sunday."

"I wonder," said Stella, "whether she understood anything she heard?"

"Possibly she might be able to give as good an account of the sermon as some other people," remarked Alick mischievously. "Come, Stella, what was the text?"

"I don't believe you know yourself," retorted Stella, coloring; and fortunately for her, Alick's attention was just then directed to the care of landing his passengers.

As they walked home, Stella and Marian in front, eagerly engrossed in a children's party which the former was describing, Lucy remarked impatiently to Alick, "How can Stella talk in that hard, unfeeling way about poor people?"

"Poor girl!" said Alick; "it is sad to see any one so spoiled by living in a cold, worldly atmosphere. As you know more of the world, Lucy, you will be more and more thankful for such a home as you have always had."

Lucy was silent. Her cousin's words made her feel that she had been indulging in self-righteous and uncharitable feelings, and she felt humbled at the lesson which she had thus received from one who did not profess to be a Christian, in one of a Christian's most important graces. But she accepted the rebuke, and she added to her evening prayer the petition that she might be made more humble and less ready to condemn; as well as that Stella's heart might be opened to receive the love of Christ, and through this of her poor earthly brothers and sisters.

The little party were soon assembled at home, and after cheerful "good-nights," Harry remarking that "he was awful tired, but there never had been a nicer picnic," the wearied excursionists soon lost all sense of fatigue in peaceful slumbers and happy dreams.

VI.

A MISSION.

> "And if this simple message
> Has now brought peace to you,
> Make known the old, old story,
> For others need it too."

TWO days after the picnic was the day fixed upon for Miss Preston's wedding, to which, as has been said, Lucy had been invited to accompany her father and aunt. Stella had not been included in the invitation, which she privately thought a great omission. It would have been such a good opportunity for showing the Ashleigh people how they dress in the city, and she felt sure that, tastefully attired in a lovely white grenadine, which would have been just the thing for the occasion, she and her dress would have added no small eclat to the wedding.

Nevertheless she behaved very amiably to Lucy, who, when she pressed her to wear one of her own pretty white dresses, and offered to lend her any of her ornaments which she fancied, felt somewhat ashamed of her own condemnatory feelings toward her cousin, since it is a very natural tendency in all of us to make our own estimate of others depend to a considerable extent upon their treatment of ourselves.

However, she adhered to her original determination of wearing the simple India muslin, which had been her own dear mother's bridal dress—its trimmings having been worked by her own hands—and all Stella's representations that it was "old-fashioned," failed to produce any effect. She would indeed have felt it treason to admit its inferiority to any of her cousin's more stylish dresses. But to please Stella, she accepted the loan of a sash pressed upon her by her cousin, who took a considerable amount of trouble in the arrangement of her toilet, and in weaving, with innate skill, a graceful wreath of delicate pink rosebuds and green leaves, which she fastened on

Lucy's dark hair, and pronounced the effect "charming," while Alick complimented her on her skill. Lucy was conscious of looking better than she had ever done before. It made her think just a little too much about her appearance, and then she felt humbled at seeing in herself the germ of the very feeling she had despised in her cousin.

The wedding arrangements were very quiet and simple. Lucy, who had never been present on so important an occasion, enjoyed it very much, notwithstanding her sorrow at parting with her teacher, whom she thought the very ideal of a bride, in her simple bridal-dress. Its simplicity, indeed, would probably have scandalized Stella, but Miss Preston was not going to be rich, or mingle in gay society, and she wisely thought show and finery quite out of place. But she had long made it her chief aim to possess that best ornament of "a meek and quiet spirit," which, we are told, "in the sight of God is of great price."

Before her departure, she took Lucy apart to say a few words of loving counsel.

"I hope you will try to work for Christ,

dear Lucy," she said, "as he gives you opportunity. Remember, a Christian who does not work is only half a Christian. Now, I think if you tried, you might do Nelly Connor some good. She wants a friend very much, and is easily won by kindness."

"I should be glad to do anything I could," said Lucy; "but what would be best to try?"

"Well, poor Nelly can't read a word, you know, and I am afraid her stepmother would not spare her to go to school. But suppose you were to get her to come to you for half an hour a day. I think her mother might be induced to let her do that. And a short reading-lesson every day would soon bring her on."

Lucy was a little disappointed. It seemed such commonplace drudgery, to drill an untaught child in the alphabet and spelling-book. Her vague idea of "work for Christ" had been of a more exalted nature. But her friend added: "I do n't mean that you should not teach her better things, also. You could, little by little, teach her a good deal about Christ in the course of your daily lessons.

But sometimes we may serve him best by doing his commonest work; and think what you will do for this poor child by putting it in her power to read the Bible for herself, and have access at all times to our Saviour's own words."

Lucy willingly promised to try, and then Mrs. Harris, as Miss Preston was now called, bade her an affectionate farewell, before going to exchange the parting words with the members of her own family. Lucy watched by the gate till she saw the carriage drive off, and then overcome by the reaction from the excitement of the occasion, hurried home through the quiet shady lane, and disregarding Stella's call, never stopped till she reached her own room.

There the astonished Stella found her lying on her bed, crying bitterly, and asked in alarm the cause of her distress. That the parting from a Sunday-school teacher, a friend so much older than herself, could have called forth such emotion, Stella could not comprehend; and it was difficult for Lucy to explain it to so unsympathetic a listener.

"Why, I'm sure I sha'n't cry so when Sophy is married and goes south, a great deal farther away than Miss Preston. Now tell me how she was dressed."

"O Stella! I can't just now," sobbed Lucy, whose crying was partly the result of nervous excitement, as well as of her realizing for the first time Miss Preston's departure. And Stella finding her attempts to soothe her unavailing, returned to her story book, until the arrival of Mrs. Steele, whom she found more communicative.

"And where is Lucy?" inquired her aunt, after satisfying Stella's curiosity. "She must have slipped away very quietly."

"Oh, she's in her own room. She was crying so, it was no use to speak to her. I don't know what for."

"She is very fond of her teacher, and I don't wonder at her crying on losing her. She is a great loss to us all."

"What a fuss they all *do* make over her. I'm sure she did n't seem anything particular," thought Stella, as she accompanied Mrs. Steele up stairs. Lucy had fallen asleep, but awoke on their entrance, and started up to arrange her disordered dress and hair before going to tea.

"Just look how you have crushed your nice dress now," exclaimed Stella, reproachfully, "and the wreath, too! It might have been fresh all the evening. You might have taken them off if you wanted to lie down."

"I did n't think of it," said Lucy apologetically, somewhat remorseful for not having treated the result of Stella's labor with more respect. "But I should n't have worn it all the evening, at any rate, for after tea I am going to see Nelly Connor."

"What, that girl we saw in the wood? What are you going to see her for?" exclaimed Stella.

"Miss Preston—I mean Mrs. Harris—wants me to try to get her to come to learn to read, if papa and aunt Mary have no objection, and I'm sure they wont."

It was to Stella a bewildering phenomenon, that Lucy should really go out of her way to invite such a girl to the house. However, partly from curiosity, and partly from having nothing better to do, she acceded to Lucy's invitation to accompany her, and after tea the girls set off, Mrs. Steele warning Lucy to be very conciliatory to Mrs. Connor, or she would not accomplish her object.

They soon reached the side of the green slope on the river bank, on which the Connors' cottage stood, and were following the path to the house, when they encountered Nelly herself, struggling up the hill with a heavy pail of water. Her brown, weather-tanned face lighted up with a glad smile when she recognized Lucy, and in reply to her inquiry, she said she was carrying up water for the next day's washing.

"And do you carry it all up from the river?" said Lucy.

"Yes, miss, every drop," replied Nelly, with a weary little sigh.

"Nelly, would you like to learn to read?" asked Lucy, plunging at once into her errand.

"I do n't know, miss," was the rather doubtful reply.

"Why, would n't you like to be able to read

that nice hymn Miss Preston gave you, for yourself?"

"Yes, miss, I'd like to be able, but I don't know if I'd like the learning."

Lucy laughed, as did Stella also, and Nelly herself.

"Well, as you can't be able to do it without learning, don't you think you'd better try?" asked Lucy.

"I don't think mother would let me, and I must hurry now, or she'll be angry at me keeping her waiting, with the baby to mind."

But just then a large dog, rushing down the hill, upset poor Nelly's pail.

"Holy Mary!" she exclaimed, using the ejaculation she had been accustomed to hear from infancy; "there's all my water spilt," and seizing her pail, she had run down to refill it, before Lucy was able to begin an intended reproof.

The girls watched her refill her pail, and return towards the cottage by a nearer though steeper path. Mrs. Connor, a tall, bony, discontented-looking woman, had come to the door to look for Nelly. Not seeing the young ladies, who were approaching the house from the other side, she screamed out in a harsh voice as Nelly approached:

"What have you been doing all this time, keeping me waiting with the child in my arms?"

"It was a dog," began Nelly, setting down her pail. But before she could finish her sentence she was roughly shaken, and sharp blows descended about her ears.

"I'll teach you to spend your time playing with dogs when I'm waiting for you. There, be off, and mind the baby;" and Nelly, putting up her hands to her face, ran crying into the house.

Lucy stood for an instant pale with indignation, and then the impulse of the moment making her forget all her aunt's warnings as to being conciliatory, and her own prudent resolves, she announced her presence by exclaiming, in a voice unsteady with emotion:

"Mrs. Connor, it's a shame to beat Nelly like that, when she hasn't been doing any harm. It was my fault she was so long, for I stopped her to speak to her, and then a dog overturned her pail."

Mrs. Connor was startled at finding there had been spectators of her violence; but she did not betray any shame she might have felt, and coolly regarding Lucy, she replied:

"Well, I don't see what business it is of yours, anyhow. If young ladies haint nothin' better to do than meddle with other folks' children, they'd better let that be!"

"What an impertinent woman!" said Stella, quite loud enough for her to hear; "Lucy, can't you come away and let her alone?"

But Lucy, though a good deal discomposed by her reception, was determined not to be easily moved from her object; and having by this time remembered her conciliatory resolve, she said, as quietly as she could:

"Mrs. Connor, my father is Mr. Raymond, the clergyman. I came to see if you would let Nelly come to our house every day, to learn to read. It's a great pity she shouldn't know how."

"I don't care who your father is," retorted the woman, in the same insolent tone. "I do n't see what you've got to do with it, whether it's a pity or not! The child's lazy enough, already, without havin' them idees put into her head, and better people than her do without book-learning."

"Lucy, do come away! I sha' n't stop to listen to her impudence," exclaimed Stella, as she turned and walked away with a haughty air. Mrs. Connor's quick eye followed her, and she half muttered to herself: "A city gal!" Then, taking up the pail which Nelly had set down, she went into the house without vouchsafing another look at Lucy, who seeing the uselessness of pressing her point, hastened to join her cousin.

"Now, you see, Lucy, you only get yourself insulted trying to do any good to such people," said Stella triumphantly. "I remember one of Sophy's friends once wanted her to go visiting poor people with her, and papa said he would n't have her go on any account; it was all nonsense running all sorts of risks to do good to people who did n't want it."

"But it was n't Mrs. Connor, but Nelly, that I wanted to do good to, and she can't help what her odious stepmother does. Only think what it must be to live with her!"

"I'd run away! But you see Nelly herself didn't seem to care about learning to read."

"Because she didn't know the good of it," replied Lucy. "But what should you or I have done, if we hadn't been made to learn, whether we liked it or not?"

"That's quite different! This girl will always have to work, I suppose, and would get on well enough without learning to read. I know mamma was always complaining that our servants were reading trashy novels, that filled their heads with nonsense and made them discontented."

"But you could have given them something better to read," suggested Lucy.

Stella said nothing in reply to this, nor did she enlighten Lucy as to the fact that in reading "trashy novels" the servants were only following their young mistresses' example. Lucy in the meantime was thinking what uphill work doing good was, and how hard it was to know how to do it. Suddenly she remembered her motto; she had been forgetting that the difficulties of the way were to be met in a strength not her own. Perhaps it was because she had not first asked for that strength, that she had met with so little success; and she regretted having so soon departed from her resolution of "looking to Jesus" in everything.

But Stella soon roused her from her "brown study," as she called it, by various questions as to Mrs. Harris' route of travel, and also as to her travelling-dress, which Lucy was very ill-prepared to answer, having cast hardly a passing glance at it, in her sorrow for her teacher's departure. On their way home, they overtook Mrs. Steele and Alick, to whom were soon related the particulars of their mission, Stella imitating Mrs. Connor's tone and manner to the life, as she graphically reproduced the conversation, much to Alick's amusement, though he ground his teeth with indignation on hearing of the violent treatment Nelly had received.

"What a woman! You mustn't leave the poor child to her tender mercies! What can she turn out, brought up under such a terma-

A MISSION.

gant? Suppose I try and bring the old lady round with a little judicious flattery?"

"I think I can manage the matter," said Mrs. Steele. "I shall make a bargain with Mrs. Connor, and promise to give her a day's work once a fortnight, provided she will let Nelly come here for half an hour every day. But do you think the child herself will be willing to come?"

"Oh, I'm sure she'll be willing to come where any one is kind to her; she has so little kindness at home," replied Lucy.

Mrs. Steele proved right. By her more judicious management and substantial inducement, Mrs. Connor was persuaded to give an ungracious assent to the plan proposed for Nelly's benefit. But, as if to be as disagreeable as possible, even in consenting, she fixed upon the time which Lucy would least have chosen for the task. The only time when she could spare Nelly, she said, was in the evening, after the children were in bed. It was the time when Lucy most enjoyed being out, watering her flowers, or taking an evening walk, or row with the others. But the choice lay between doing the work then, or not at all; and when she thought how light was the task given her to do, and how slight the sacrifice, she felt ashamed of her inclination to murmur at it.

So Nelly's education began with the alphabet; and though it was a drudgery both for teacher and pupil, reciprocal kindness and gratitude helped on the task, and before many weeks had passed, Nelly was spelling words of two syllables, and had learned some truths, at least, of far greater importance.

VII.

TEMPTATIONS

"Or rather help us, Lord, to choose the good—
To pray for naught, to seek to none but Thee
Nor by our 'daily bread' mean common food
Nor say, 'From this world's evil set us free.'"

THE Sunday-school was again assembled on another Sunday afternoon, some weeks later. The day was even warmer than the one on which our story opened, and all the church windows were opened to their widest extent to admit every breath of air which came in through the waving pine-boughs. Lucy had been promoted to teach a small class of her own, in which Nelly Connor had willingly taken her place. She was indeed advancing faster in spiritual than in secular learning, for in the first she had the best of all teachers, to whose teaching her simple heart was open—the Holy Spirit himself.

Bessie Ford had found another teacher, and beside her sat Stella, who, partly from finding her Sunday afternoons dull, and partly from feeling that it was her uncle's wish that she should accompany Lucy to Sunday-school, had overcome her objection to it so far as to go with her cousin. And having found out on the first Sunday how deficient she herself was in Bible knowledge, and never liking to appear inferior to others in anything, she took some pains to prepare her lessons at least so far that her ignorance might not lower her in the eyes of her classmates. It was a poor motive, certainly, still seeds of divine truth were gradually finding their way into her heart, which might in time germinate and bear fruit. And her stay in Mr. Raymond's household, where "serving the Lord" was avowedly the ruling principle, had already exercised a healthful influence over her impressionable nature.

On this particular Sunday the interesting announcement was made that the annual "pic-

TEMPTATIONS. 101

nic" or Sunday-school excursion was to take place on the following Wednesday, the place being a beautiful oak wood about a mile from the church in the opposite direction from Mill-Bank Farm. As little groups clustered together on leaving the church door, there was a general buzz of talk about the picnic.

Lucy stopped Nelly Connor to ask her whether she thought her mother would let her go to the picnic.

Poor Nelly looked very doubtful as she replied, "I don't know; I'm afraid not."

"Well, Nelly, I'll see what can be done about it," said Lucy encouragingly.

"But I haven't anything decent to wear to it, miss," replied Nelly, looking dolefully down on the tattered frock, which her mother never took the trouble to mend, and which she, poor child, could not except in the most bungling fashion.

Lucy walked home thoughtfully, and as the fruit of her meditation, a print dress of her own was next morning produced, and a consultation was held with her aunt as to the practicability of altering it to fit Nelly. "I only wonder I didn't think of it before," she said, "for she is always so miserably dressed. Will you help me to make it up, Stella?"

"My dear, I wouldn't know how! The most I ever sewed in my life was to hem a pocket-handkerchief."

Mrs. Steele looked shocked at such deficiency in what she rightly considered a most important part of female education. She had always taken care that Lucy should spare enough time from her more congenial studies to learn, at least, to sew neatly.

"Why, Stella!" Lucy exclaimed, "you're almost as bad as poor Nelly, who said she had never learned to sew, because 'nobody had teached her.'"

"I've never had time to learn; I like embroidery better, and mamma said we should never need to do plain sewing, so she didn't see the use of our taking up our time with it."

"No one knows what she may have to do," remarked Mrs. Steele gently. "It is always best to know how, at any rate."

"Well, I hope I shall never have to, for I should hate it!"

TEMPTATIONS. 103

However, when Lucy was fairly at work on the little frock, Stella good-naturedly offered to help her a little, though, never having been trained to perseverance in anything, her assistance was not very efficient.

Bessie Ford had gone home from Sunday-school with her head turned by hearing some foolish talk about her dress. Alas! how often it is that Sunday-scholars, on leaving the school, instead of giving one thought to the divine truths they have been hearing, allow their attention to be absorbed with the petty frivolities in which their thoughts run wild.

"Mother," said Bessie, after she had duly announced the intended picnic, "can't I have a new pink sash for my white frock? Nancy Parker is going to have ever so many new things."

"No, child," said her mother, "you don't need a new sash. Your frock looks quite well enough without one. But I've been thinking you'd be the better of a new hat: for the one you have looks a little brown. And as you've been a pretty good girl, and a deal less forgetful of late, I wouldn't mind getting you a new hat, if you'll hurry and finish up that plain sewing you've had in hand so long. It's time it was done and put away."

Bessie looked a little disappointed. The new hat was not so attractive as the sash would have been. Suddenly her mother's remark on the brownness of her hat suggested the image of Nelly's tattered, dingy one which she had noticed that afternoon.

"What would you do with my old hat, mother," she said, "if I get a new one?"

"I don't know; you've your sun-bonnet for wearing about the farm. Put it by for Jenny, perhaps," suggested the thrifty Mrs. Ford.

"Might I give it to Nelly Connor, mother? Hers will hardly stay together."

Mrs. Ford had never seen Nelly, but she knew something of her forlorn situation. "I'm sure," she said, "I shouldn't mind if you did. I dare say it would be charity to her, poor thing." And it occurred to her to think whether she, a well-to-do farmer's wife, had been as abundant in deeds of charity as she might have been.

Bessie considered the matter settled, and next day set to work with renewed zeal on the "plain sewing" which had been getting on very languidly, for Bessie was not fond of long straight seams, or of sitting still for any length of time. She set herself a task, as she took her seat under the spreading butternut-tree; and Jenny and Jack came to beg for "a story." Bessie's story-telling powers had been largely developed of late to make the Sunday lessons she had begun to give the restless little things more palatable to them. Only the promise of "a story" could fix their attention long enough to commit to memory a simple verse. And her powers once found out, she soon had demands upon her for stories to a greater extent than her patience was always equal to satisfying.

Bessie had become, as her mother had noticed, much more thoughtful of late. Her card, hung up in her room, kept always before her mind her resolution to "look to Jesus" for help to live to please him. And though she still often forgot and yielded to temptation, yet, on the whole, she was steadily advancing in that course in which all must be either going forward or backward. Her mother noticed that this decided improvement dated from the day when she had brought home the card; a day which had not been without influence on herself; although when worldly principles have been long suffered to hold undisputed sway, it is difficult at once to overcome old habits; and lost ground is not less hard to retrieve in spiritual than in earthly things.

Bessie was still diligently working at her "task," when she saw Nancy Parker running up across the fields.

"O Bessie," she said breathlessly, "get ready and come right away. My cousins have come to spend the day, and we're going boating up the river, and then home to supper. The rest are all waiting in the boat down there, and I ran up to get you. So be quick!"

Bessie hesitated. If she went with Nancy, a considerable portion of the work she had set herself to do would be left undone. Besides, her mother had gone to Ashleigh, leaving her in charge; and Bessie was not at all sure that, had she been at home, she would approve of her joining the party.

To be sure, she could not be absolutely certain of her mother's disapproval, and she could easily run down for Sam to come and stay with the children. At the worst, she did not think her mother would be much displeased, and the thought of the pleasant row, and the merry party, and all the "fun" they would have, offered no small temptation.

"Quick, Bessie!" Nancy urged, impatient of her delay.

"I don't think I can go, Nancy; mother's out, and I've a lot of sewing to do."

"Bother the sewing! Your mother wouldn't mind, I'm sure. Mine lets me do exactly as I like. Come and get ready;" and she pulled Bessie from her seat, and drew her, half-resisting, towards the house.

They went up stairs together, Bessie feeling far from satisfied with herself for yielding where conscience told her she ought not to yield.

"My!" said Nancy, whose quick eyes had been glancing round the room; "what a grand ticket you've got hanging up there. Where did you get it?"

Bessie's eye turned to her motto, and she stood for a minute looking at it in silence. Then, instead of replying to the question, she said, "Nancy, I cannot go; it wouldn't be right."

"Well, that's a nice way to treat me!" said Nancy angrily. "After my waiting so long, too. Why, don't you know your own mind? Come, you can't change now; I'm not going to be cheated, after all my trouble."

"I'm very sorry, Nancy, but I oughtn't to have said I would go at all. Don't wait any longer; but I'll go down to the boat with you."

"Oh, don't trouble yourself; I can do without your company." And off she ran, before Bessie could say any more.

Bessie felt sorry at having vexed Nancy, and thought a little wistfully of the afternoon's pleasure that she might have had. But she felt satisfied that she had done right, and felt thankful that she had had strength given to resist a temptation to which she now felt she would have done very wrong to yield. So she went back to her shady seat with a light heart, and stitched away diligently, not repining although she heard the merry voices of the party, borne to her from the river.

As her mother had not returned by the time her task was completed, she went in and got tea ready, and then calling up two of the gentlest cows, she had milked them by the time Mrs. Ford appeared, tired and dusty from her long walk. Her pleased surprise at Bessie's thoughtful industry in getting through so much of the work which she thought was still before her, was in itself sufficient reward for the self-denial, and Bessie felt what a shame it would have been if her mother, fatigued as she was, had had everything to do on her return, while *she* was away on a pleasure party.

Of course Mrs. Ford was soon informed of Nancy's visit and invitation. "Oh, my child!" she exclaimed, "I am so glad you refused to go. Mrs. Thompson, in the village, was just telling me about these cousins of Nancy's, and says they are the wildest set in Burford, and that their society wouldn't do Nancy any good. So if you had gone I should have been very sorry. I'm so glad you did n't."

How glad Bessie was that she had been enabled to resist the temptation. But she felt she could not take the credit to herself; so she said:

"I had the greatest mind to go, mother, but something told me I should n't, just as I was almost going."

"Well, it's all the same to me, as you did n't go. And you were a real good girl, Bessie, to stay!"

What a safeguard is a definite duty conscientiously pursued. If Bessie had not had her task of sewing to finish, with the feeling that it was her duty to do it, she might have been more easily led away against her better judgment.

Nelly Connor had had her temptation, too, the same evening. Her mother had sent her to take home some clothes she had been washing; and as Nelly was carrying the basket she noticed a pretty pink printed frock lying on the top, which looked as if it would exactly fit her. How nice it would be, she thought, if she had such a frock to wear to the picnic! Then came one of the evil suggestions which the tempter is so ready to put into the heart: what if she should keep it till the picnic was over, and wear it just that once? She could hide it and put it on somewhere out of her stepmother's sight; and then, perhaps, if she were dressed so nicely, some of the other little girls might be willing to play with her; for the poor child felt her isolated position.

Then conscience said, "Would it be right?" Had she not been learning, "Thou shalt not steal"? And had not Miss Lucy explained to her that that meant taking anything, even the least, that was not her own? A short time ago Nelly would have appropriated any trifle that came in her way without thinking twice about it; but some light had visited her mind now, and she could distinguish what was darkness. But then, this would not be stealing, it would only be borrowing the frock! At last, she was so near the house that she was obliged to make up her mind at once; so scarcely giving herself time to think, she wrapped up the frock in the smallest possible compass, hid it behind a stone, and ran on to leave her basket, hurrying nervously back, lest some one should inquire for the missing article.

She found it quite safe, however, and managed to convey it unseen to her little attic-room. But Nelly felt far more unhappy than she had ever been when her harsh mother had beaten her most severely. She could not understand how it was that she should feel so miserable. She was glad that she could not go for her lesson to-night, for she should have been ashamed to face Miss Lucy. One of the children just then began to cry, and she ran down stairs, glad of something to do, and took the utmost pains to do her evening work particularly well, by way of making up for the wrong of which she was inwardly conscious.

But when she went to bed, Nelly, for the first time in her life, tossed about, unable to sleep. All sorts of possibilities of detection and disgrace occurred to her, and above all, the voice of conscience told her she was little better than a thief. She had knelt down to say the simple prayer she had been first

TEMPTATIONS. 113

taught by Miss Preston: "O Lord, take away my sin, and make me thy child, for Jesus Christ's sake," but indulged sin had come between her and the Father to whom she prayed, so that her prayer was only a formal one. She fell asleep at last, but only to dream uneasy dreams, in which the pink frock was always prominent: and when she awoke in the early morning it was with an uneasy sense of something wrong, soon defined into a distinct recollection. As she lay watching the early sunbeams slanting golden into her dingy attic, her eye fell upon the card, pinned up against the wall, "LOOKING UNTO JESUS," which she could now spell out herself. Had she not been told to "look to Jesus" when unhappy or naughty, and he would deliver her? She knew now that she could speak to Jesus anywhere; so springing out of bed and kneeling down, she simply but heartily asked him to help her to be good. Then, putting on her clothes with all the haste she could, for fear she might be tempted to change her mind, she ran off unobserved, carrying with her the coveted frock, which she handed, without a word, to the servant who was sweeping the steps, and who, recognizing her, supposed her stepmother had forgotten to send it home with the rest of the washing.

Nelly ran off with a heart so much lighter that she did not mind even the box on the ear which she received on her return for being out "idling about," instead of lighting the fire for the breakfast. She felt she had deserved much more than that, and she contentedly accepted it as a slight punishment for her wrong-doing.

That day, when Mrs. Connor was working at Mr. Raymond's, Mrs. Steele, showing her the frock which was now completed, told her it was to be given to Nelly on condition of her being allowed to go to the picnic. Mrs. Connor of course grumbled a good deal about the inconvenience of having to spare Nelly for a whole afternoon, but the frock tempted her, and reflecting that the opportune arrival of this frock would do away with any necessity for getting Nelly a new one for a long time to come, she ungraciously gave her consent that she should go.

When Nelly came that evening for her lesson, Lucy gladly informed her that she was to be allowed to go to the picnic, and presented her with the frock which had been provided for her. Lucy was prepared for her look of surprise, but not so for her covering her face with her hands and bursting into tears. With some trouble she drew from her a confused account of the cause of her trouble—the sin she had been led into, and which touched her generous nature all the more, now that the frock she had been wishing for was so opportunely provided.

Lucy was at first somewhat shocked that Nelly had been capable of taking such a liberty with what was not her own, not being able to realize the strength of such a temptation to a child whose possessions were so few, and she privately resolved not to tell Stella, who would scarcely have thought how nobly she overcame the temptation.

However, she commended and encouraged Nelly, and told her always to resort to the same sure Helper in time of temptation, and to do it in the first place; "and Jesus is always ready to hear and help you," she added.

"An' it was Him told you to give me the frock too, wasn't it? And I'm rightly thankful to Him and you too, Miss Lucy."

And Nelly carried home her new acquisition with very different feelings from those with which she had taken the frock she had coveted.

"How glad I am I thought of getting it ready for her," thought Lucy as she watched her depart, her own heart full of the pleasure of doing a much-needed kindness; the only drawback being her regret that Nelly had not a new hat likewise.

The much-watched-for day on which the picnic was to be held turned out as fine as the most eager young hearts could desire, notwithstanding one or two slight showers that fell in the early morning. But these only cleared the air and laid the dust and made the foliage so fresh and glistening that its early summer beauty seemed for a time revived.

The fine old oak grove where the feast was to be held was, even before the appointed hour, astir with bright little groups of happy children. The teachers and some of the elder girls were already busy at a roughly-constructed table, unpacking and arranging cups and saucers, filling the latter with the ripe-red berries which had been brought in in great abundance, and cutting up the piles of buns and cakes. Bessie Ford was superintending the distribution of the cream which had come in large jars from the farm-houses, and of which Mill-Bank Farm had contributed the richest and finest. Lucy of course was among the working-party, her position as Mr. Raymond's daughter giving her a degree of importance far from disagreeable to her. Stella, seated with her friend Marian Wood in the centre of a mass of flowers, was daintily arranging them in tiny bouquets to be given to the children.

At last Bessie, who with Nelly's new hat beside her had been watching the various arrivals, descried the little solitary figure with its dark, hanging locks, for which she had been looking. When she approached her, she was quite surprised at the change in her appearance produced by the fresh, pretty frock; and when her old hat was removed, and the new one placed upon her dark hair, which had been smoothly combed and brushed out and put back from her eyes, she really looked as nice as most of the children there. Her dark eyes danced with pleasure as Bessie, herself almost as happy, took her to a group of girls about her own age, and introduced her to them as a stranger, to whom they must try to make the picnic as pleasant as possible. Bessie was a favorite with all the girls, and they willingly promised what she asked, so that Nelly, for the first time in many months, had a really good game of play with children of her own age, an intense pleasure to her social, kindly Irish nature, which, with her ready wit, soon made her the life of the little group.

Two or three hours passed rapidly by. Lucy and Bessie went from one part of the ground to another, encouraging the little ones to run and romp, bringing forward shy or isolated children, and watching that the ruder and stronger did not oppress the weaker, or sitting down to talk with some of the older girls, who preferred a quiet chat. Stella in her airy muslin flounces, a tiny hat with floating blue ribbons crowning her golden tresses, flitted about with a winning grace which made her the admired of all observers. She felt herself a sort of princess on the occasion, and as she dearly loved popularity, even among rustics, she spared no pains to be affable and agreeable, and felt quite rewarded when she heard such speeches as, " What a sweet, pretty young lady Miss Lucy's cousin is." " Is n't she, for all the world, just like a picture?"

Alick watched with some amusement the patronizing air which mingled with her affability, and perhaps added to her consequence with those who could not appreciate the higher beauty of simplicity of manner. Lucy could not repress a slight feeling of annoyance at seeing how easily her cousin won her way, and how far her more adventitious advantages threw into the shade her own real exertions for the pleasure of those around her. Not that the exertions had been prompted by a desire for praise; but she was not yet unselfish enough to be satisfied that they had gained the desired end, although not fully appreciated by those for whom they had been made. The difference between the cousins was, that

Lucy liked approbation, when she did what was right for its own sake, while Stella's conduct was chiefly prompted by the desire of admiration.

"Lucy," said Stella, coming up to her during the afternoon, "do you see that ridiculous imitation of my dress that Nancy Parker has on? I suppose she wanted to be dressed just like me; but I'm glad I wore a different one to-day." Yet, though Stella professed some annoyance, she was secretly a little flattered at Nancy's thus recognizing her as a leader of fashion.

Alick and Harry were invaluable aids in promoting the enjoyment of the boys, as was Fred, also, in his quieter way. Towards the close of the afternoon Mr. Raymond appeared, and after a pleasant greeting interchanged with his older parishioners present, the children assembled in the centre of the ground to listen to a few kind and earnest words from their pastor. He took as his subject the "remembering their Creator in the days of their youth;" and after reminding them to whom they owed the innocent pleasures which had

TEMPTATIONS. 121

been provided for them, he spoke earnestly of the Creator and Redeemer they were to "remember," to whom they should now bring their young hearts, that he might take them and make them his. The sunshine of his gracious presence would, he said, hallow and sweeten their joyous hours, and be a stay and support even when the "evil days" should come, and all other sources of happiness should fail them. His address was not so long as to weary even the most impatient, and when it was concluded, the children stood up and sang a hymn, which, to Nelly's great delight, was her favorite—"I lay my sins on Jesus." Then, after Mr. Raymond had briefly asked a blessing on the food of which they were about to partake, and the intercourse they had had, and were still to have, the children quietly dispersed into little groups and sat down on the grass to enjoy the good things that were liberally provided for them.

The distribution kept the assistants busy, and some care had to be exercised lest too large a share of the cakes should be appropriated by some of the more greedy; alas that there should be such among Sunday-school children! Nelly Connor had seldom had a treat in her life, but she would not for the world have taken one cake more than her share, or have hidden one away in her pocket, as she saw some better-dressed children doing.

At last, when the dew was beginning to moisten the grass, and the fast lengthening shadows told that the long summer-day was drawing to a close, a bell sounded to collect the children, and after singing the evening hymn, and having been commended by Mr. Raymond to the care of Him who neither slumbers nor sleeps, all quietly dispersed to their homes. The "picnic" so eagerly looked forward to, was over, as all earthly pleasures must sooner or later be. Not a single incident had marred its harmony, and to Nelly Connor in particular the day had been one of unmingled and unprecedented enjoyment. How different from what it would have been, had she not, in a strength from above, overcome the temptation to which she had so nearly yielded.

VIII.

PARTINGS.

"Only, since our souls will shrink
At the touch of natural grief,
When our earthly loved ones sink,
Lend us, Lord, thy sure relief—
Patient hearts, their pain to see,
And thy grace, to follow thee."

STELLA'S visit was now drawing to a close. She had very much enjoyed its novelty, and had during her stay made some acquisitions, though not of a kind that she yet appreciated or was even conscious of. It was impossible for her to be so long in a household where every day was begun and closed by invoking God's presence and guidance; where his blessing and approbation were steadily regarded as the best of all good;

where the standard of action was that laid down in his word; and where his strengthening grace was looked upon as the most necessary equipment for daily life, without receiving a deeper impression of the importance of these things, than she had ever before felt. And though the members of her uncle's family had their share of human imperfections, yet on the whole, the example she had seen around her had been sufficiently consistent to show her, almost against her will, the beauty of a Christian life, as contrasted with one based wholly on worldly principles. Some seeds of good, at all events, she carried back with her, though she was far from having profited, as she might have done, had her heart been more open to receive the influences around her.

It had been a new thing to Lucy to have a companion of her own age and sex; she had become really attached to her winsome cousin, and all the transient irritation which Stella had often caused her passed into oblivion now that they were really about to part. Alick was to escort Stella to the residence of a friend whom she was to visit on her way home; and the cousins parted with affectionate hopes of a visit from Stella next summer, and also of a winter visit which Mr. Raymond had half promised that Lucy should make to her cousin's city home.

The loss of Stella's restless and vivacious presence made no small blank in the house— a blank to be still further increased by the permanent departure of Alick soon after his return from escorting Stella. He had at last decided on the place in which he was to settle—a new and rising village in the far West— and had already been claiming his mother's promise, that so soon as he should be able to provide a home for her, she would come and preside in it. Mrs. Steele felt that it would be her duty to comply with her son's desire, and Mr. Raymond, while very sorry to lose his sister's kind, motherly supervision of his family, felt that he could not dissuade her from an arrangement so right and natural, and to which he had long looked forward as a probability. However, she was not to leave them for some months at least, and during that time Lucy was to learn all she could about housekeeping, in order to be able to fill her aunt's place as well as a young beginner could do.

To Lucy, indeed, there mingled with her regret for her aunt's expected departure, a certain latent satisfaction at the increased importance of her own place in the household; and her ambition was so much stimulated by the hope of fulfilling her new duties in the most exemplary manner, that it somewhat alleviated her sorrow at the thought of losing the kind aunt who had filled a mother's place.

Many were the regrets when the time came for Alick's final departure from Ashleigh to his distant sphere of duty; and Mr. Raymond, in bidding him a kind farewell, added in an earnest tone the not unneeded admonition: "Alick, my boy, don't forget who says, 'Seek ye first the kingdom of God and his righteousness, and all other things shall be added unto you.'"

And so the happy party, who had enjoyed together at Ashleigh the pleasant summer days, were scattered, never again to meet there under the same circumstances. For the autumn, bringing the cold blasts and nipping frosts that scattered the rich summer foliage and made the earth bleak and bare, brought other changes, far sadder than these.

Nelly was the first to whose life came a sudden change. A rumor reached the village that a deck-hand on one of the river steamers had lost his life by a fatal accident, and that the man's name was Michael Connor. It seldom happens that such reports turn out groundless, and when Mrs. Connor, having heard of it, hastened to the wharf to discover what truth there might be in it, she met a comrade of her husband's who had come to announce to his family the sad fact.

Mrs. Connor did not profess any deep regret for a husband whom she had often asserted to be a good-for-nothing scamp. She looked at the matter chiefly in a pecuniary point of view, and on making a rapid calculation came to the conclusion that any deficiency caused by the loss of the small fraction of his earnings that came into her possession would be more than made up by her being relieved of the maintenance of Nelly, for whom she did not consider it her duty any longer to provide.

But in Nelly herself, Michael Connor had at least one true mourner. She forgot all her father's carelessness and neglect, and remembered only that he was her father, who used in days long past, when her mother was alive, to take her on his knee and call her his "darlint." When it broke fully on her mind that she should never see him again—that he had left her for ever, as her mother had done—her grief for a while knew no control. Poor child, she had literally no one in the world "belonging to her," so far as she knew, and she felt utterly desolate and forlorn. Finding but little comfort at home, where her new mother's cold, unfeeling remarks only aggravated her sorrow, she betook herself to Lucy, who had just heard, with great concern, of Nelly's bereavement. She did her best to comfort her, and though at first the kind words only seemed to make the tears flow faster, by degrees the child was soothed and calmed, and able to listen to Mr. Raymond when he laid his hand kindly on her head and told her that she must look to God as her Father now, and must go and "tell Jesus" all her troubles. Then he made her repeat after him the verse, "When my father and my mother forsake me, then the Lord will take me up."

"But, Miss Lucy," said Nelly, as she was going away, "where is it I'm going to live now?"

"Why, is your mother going away?"

"Niver a bit, miss, but she says she's kept me long enough now, and she wont keep me any longer."

Lucy could scarcely believe that this could be more than one of Mrs. Connor's meaningless threats, and tried to reässure Nelly that it would be all right. But Mrs. Steele, knowing Mrs. Connor's hard, selfish nature, was by no means so sure that there might not be something in it, and was not surprised when she appeared next day to say that she thought Nelly's grand friends might do something for her, now her poor father was gone, and she had no one to look to her.

"But she has you, of course," Mrs. Steele replied. "We shall be very glad to help you as far as possible, but you have shown yourself well able to support your family."

"She ain't one of my family," replied Mrs. Connor, "and I've kept her long enough for all the good I've ever got out of her, so I don't see that it's any of my business to take the bit out of my children's mouths and put it into hers."

Mrs. Connor would probably not have come to this decision had she not been less dependent than formerly on Nelly's assistance. But as her youngest child was now able to run alone, and the eldest could, on an emergency, take care of the rest, and as she now took in most of her washing, she had less need for an additional worker, involving an additional mouth to be fed. Besides, Nelly was a "growing girl," she reflected, and would be always costing her more for food and clothing, so that to be rid of her maintenance would be so much clear gain. She was therefore inexorable in her determination that Nelly should not remain with her, unless, indeed, the ladies would pay for her board—a proposition which Mrs. Steele declined to entertain.

It was taken seriously into consideration by Lucy and her aunt what could be done to provide Nelly with a home. Lucy was eager that she should be at once taken into their own household, to be trained for domestic service, but this Mrs. Steele thought impracticable at present, as she knew that their own busy, capable handmaid would strongly object to have her time taken up in teaching a girl who would give her so much additional trouble.

"But there are other people," she said, "who would be very glad of a child like Nelly, who would cost nothing for wages, to train and make useful. I am going to Mill-Bank Farm this afternoon to see about some butter, and I'll see if Mrs. Ford knows of any one who would take her."

Lucy assented rather reluctantly. It would have been so nice, she thought, to have her protégée immediately under her own charge, to teach and train into a model servant. She had not yet learned the distrust in her own powers which experience gives, and she saw only the bright side of the plan, not the difficulties in its execution.

Mrs. Ford's motherly heart was at once roused to pity for the little orphan's forlorn condition, and to indignation at Mrs. Connor's heartless conduct.

"After all the work she's got out of her, too!" she said; "making that poor child drudge away morning, noon, and night. I'm sure she's been worth a deal more to her than the little bit of meat and drink she's given her—with a grudge, as I hear from the neighbors. Well, well! it's a queer world!"

Mrs. Ford promised to try to find out a good place for Nelly, and early next morning she made her appearance, having taken the long walk on one of her busiest days, in order to "talk over Nelly's business," as she said. She proposed to take the orphan into her own family, for a time at least, until some more permanent situation should turn up. "We'll never miss the little she'll want," she said; "and if we did, I've been often thinking of late that we've been too much taken up with doing the most we could for this world, and been caring too little for the poor that our Saviour says are to be always with us. So my mind would be easier if I were doing this much, at any rate, and the poor thing 'll be more likely to get a good, steady place if I take her in hand and teach her a bit myself."

So it was settled, and Nelly, to her surprise and delight, found herself an inmate, for a time at least, of Mill-Bank Farm, though she was made to understand that the arrangement was not a permanent one. The present comfort and happiness were enough for her, however, for she was not given to spoiling the enjoyments of to-day by thoughts about the morrow; and she certainly had never, so far as her recollection went, been half so happy as she now was under Mrs. Ford's motherly care, with Bessie for a half-companion, half-teacher, and removed from the sound of the harsh words and tones which had so long been the constant accompaniments of her life.

One of Mrs. Ford's first cares was to provide her with some needed clothing, from Bessie's out-grown garments, which otherwise would have been stowed thriftily away for little Jenny. Lucy added her contribution for the same object, and it was considered a good opportunity for teaching her what she so much needed to learn—plain sewing. Mrs. Ford, who was a capital seamstress, as well as housewife, undertook to make Nelly a good needlewoman, if she would be diligent in trying to learn; and she was too grateful and too anxious to please not to try her best, though the long, tedious seams often tried her restless, active spirit. When she found herself getting so impatient that she felt as if she could not sit still any longer, or, at any rate, could not force herself to do the work with patience and care, she would remember the injunction to "tell Jesus" her troubles and difficulties, and the restless spirit would become quiet, and the strength to fulfil her good resolutions would come back. As it was too far for her to go to Lucy now for her daily lessons, Lucy resigned her to Bessie's tuition, though somewhat unwillingly, for her teaching had become a source of real pleasure to her, and she felt that in it she was doing some definite work for her Saviour. She had not yet got into the habit of looking upon everything she was called in duty to do, as work done for Christ, just in proportion as it was done in a spirit of cheerful faith and dependence, "looking unto Jesus" both as the master and the friend.

But dark days were at hand for Lucy too, days when she would need all the support her faith could give. Mr. Raymond's never robust constitution had been for some time gradually failing, though Lucy, seeing him daily, and accustomed to consider her father "not very strong," had not observed it. Late in November, a long, cold drive in sleet and rain to visit a dying parishioner, brought on symptoms of fever, which rapidly increased, till the doctor, who had been summoned to attend him, looked very anxious, and pronounced his patient in a most critical condition. Lucy had been so long accustomed to his occasional illnesses that she was slow to admit the idea of danger to her father, the possibility of losing whom had scarcely ever occurred to her mind. Therefore, though she could not help seeing her aunt's extreme anxiety, she resolutely turned her thoughts to the happier prospect of her father's recovery, when he would again occupy his wonted place, and the house would be like itself again.

Even when Mr. Raymond's extreme weakness forced the others to give up hope, Lucy still hoped and prayed, by the sick-bed and in her own chamber, as she had never prayed before. Surely, she thought, if she prayed humbly and earnestly her prayer would not be denied by Him who has said, "Ask and ye shall receive;" and her father would be restored to her. She did not consider that as regards earthly things the promise must be limited, or the conditions of human life would have to be altered. If our prayers that our dear ones should be spared to us were always to be granted, when would they ever attain that blessed rest in the Father's house, the haven they have been looking for through all the cares and troubles of their mortal pilgrimage?

Mr. Raymond had often longed for the time when his earthly work should be done, and he should be called to the presence of his Saviour, to reunion with his early-lost wife. And now, though in the unconsciousness of his exhausted powers he knew it not, that time had come.

His "falling asleep" was as peaceful as the sinking of a child into its nightly slumber, and Lucy did not realize that it was death till, in the dark December morning, she stood by the cold, white couch on which lay the inanimate form to which, from her earliest days, she had always looked as her protector and guide. It was hard to persuade herself that that cold form was not her father; but that all that had made the living, sentient being had passed to another state of existence beyond her power to follow, beyond her power to conceive! In the strange awe that came upon her, she lost for a time the sense of the desolation of her bereavement—lost all thought for herself in trying to pierce the darkness which hung between her and the "undiscovered lands," in which both her parents now were. With Fred it was much the same: an awe-struck solemnity at first repressing in both the natural feeling of personal loss. Harry was the only one whose bitter childish grief broke forth uncontrolled.

But there was time in the blank, desolate days that followed to realize the full bitterness of the bereavement. Once out of the still, solemn chamber, which seemed to hush all violent emotion, there were associations at every step, in every room, of him whose place should know him no more, to call forth the uncontrollable agony of tears that had for a time been repressed. And when the still form had been carried to its last resting-place, and the heavy consciousness made itself felt that he was gone, never in any possible event to return to them, it seemed to Lucy as if it would have been too terrible to bear but for the Saviour, to whom she carried her grief, and found that, though He does not always at our asking restore our sick to this mortal life, yet that, when He takes them away, He can and will be a very present "help in time of trouble."

But there was already another grief looming darkly in the distance, which Lucy almost shrank from facing. The home that had been hers from her birth, must be broken up. The external surroundings in which her life had been always set, were to be torn from it, and any other phase of life seemed as if it must be a dreary blank. She could not then realize the possibility of ever forming new associations, or taking root in any other home. And, indeed, it is doubtful whether one ever does take root again, in the same sense as in the home of childhood, which is linked with the earliest associations of opening thought, and with all the hallowed ties that cluster around a child's happy home. Other houses are but places of abode, made home by association; *that* seemed absolutely and in itself *home.*

Alick had come to Ashleigh as soon as possible after his uncle's death, and was anxious to take his mother at once to the new home he had been preparing for her. As to Lucy, there seemed to be but one course advisable. As Mr. Raymond could leave only a very slender provision for his family, he had always been anxious that Lucy should have an education sufficiently thorough to put her in a position to gain her own livelihood by teaching, and a way seemed opened for her to carry out his wishes in this respect. Mr. Brooke, urged thereto by his daughter Stella, had written to Mrs. Steele, offering to receive Lucy into his own family for the next two or three years, in order to give her the advantage of a first-class education, which was, he remarked, "the best he could do for her, as it would give her the ability to do for herself."

Lucy shrank from the prospect of so long a residence in a home so unlike the one she was leaving, as from Stella's remarks she felt sure it must be. But to go, with Harry, to live with Mrs. Steele and Alick, as they kindly invited her to do, in case she could not make up her mind to go to Mr. Brooke's, would, she felt, be imposing far too great a burden on Alick's kindness, though it seemed just the right home for Harry. Fred, who had been summoned from college to his father's death-bed, must return to resume his theological studies, for they all insisted that he should not think of giving up the career which had been his father's desire for him as well as his own. The more Lucy thought about the matter, the more distinctly she saw that there was no other way rightly open to her, especially as, even could she think it right to accompany Mrs. Steele and Alick, she could not, in the new village in the West, expect any educational advantages. But it was with much reluctance, and after many prayers to be strengthened to meet the new experiences before her, that she gave her decision to go to live for the present in her cousin Stella's home.

Fred, to whom she confided her extreme shrinking from venturing into an atmosphere which her fancy pictured as so cold and uncongenial, endeavored to reassure her by reminding her, of what she knew indeed, but found it difficult to realize, that her Saviour could be as near her in the crowded city, as in her quiet country home, since his love is

"A flower that cannot die
For lack of leafy screen:"

and that it was a sickly Christianity which must necessarily fade and droop when removed from the atmosphere in which it had been originally nurtured.

"Well," she said at last, disconsolately, "it doesn't matter so very much! I can never be very happy again, now papa is gone, and the best thing is to think most about the home he has gone to, and try to follow him there."

Something of this kind she wrote to her old friend and teacher, Mrs. Harris, who had sent her a letter of loving sympathy. She smiled half sadly when she read Lucy's disconsolate reply. Mrs. Harris had seen enough of life to know that a young heart is not permanently depressed by a first grief, and she feared for Lucy, if she should trust to the influence of sorrow alone to keep her "unspotted from the world."

"My dear Lucy," she wrote, "while it is well that you should always cherish your dear father's memory, and keep his counsels and his example always with you as a protecting influence, beware of trusting too much to this. He himself would have told you that it is not him you are to follow, but Him whom he followed, 'Jesus Christ, the same yesterday, to-day, and for ever.' This alone can be our strength. Time is strong against our deepest sorrow, and no influence can permanently hold, except the constraining love of Christ.

Never lose the habit of looking steadily to him, and to him alone, for daily and hourly strength."

It was wise counsel, and Lucy, in time, came to find out how true it was.

It is needless to dwell upon the pain of the breaking up; the packing up and stowing away treasured possessions, so closely associated with the times now passed away, the sorrowful leave-takings of old friends who felt as if they were losing the last link with their beloved minister in the departure of his family; the sad farewell looks at all the well-known home objects: the flower-beds, the gravel walk, the shrubs and trees, every twig of which had such a familiar look. Many a time it seemed as if it must be only a sad dream, that all these things were about to pass from her daily life into a vision of memory. Happily it was winter; had it been in the fair flush of summer, when her home looked its loveliest, the parting would have been far harder. As it was, it was hard enough; but she tried to conceal her sorrow from those to whose pain it would have added, though many a tear was secretly shed over even the old gray cat, and the gentle, petted cow, which were almost home friends.

At last all the preparations were completed. The house, stripped of most of its familiar furnishings, wore already a strange, uncomfortable aspect, full of packing cases and confusion. Fred had already been obliged to return to college, and Lucy was to be the next to go. Alick was to escort her to the next railway station, and see her on the train which was to take her to the city. It was the first time she had ever travelled alone, and she rather dreaded it; but she knew that it would be very inconvenient for Alick to accompany her the whole way, and she would not admit that she thought the solitary journey at all a formidable one.

Poor Nelly, who grieved as much for her friend's departure as she had done for her father's death, came on the last morning to say good-by, although Lucy had already taken leave of her and Bessie at Mill-Bank Farm, and had made the latter promise to write to her sometimes.

PARTINGS.

"And it's sorry I am, Miss Lucy, you're going, and you so good to me," sobbed Nelly, when she felt the parting moment was really come.

"Well, Nelly, we must both try to remember our Friend in heaven, who has been so good to us both. You love him, I hope, Nelly, and pray to him always?"

"Indeed I do, and I always pray God to bless you, Miss Lucy."

"Well, I wont forget to pray for you, Nelly, and we know he will hear our prayers," replied Lucy kindly.

Acts of Christian kindness often bring their reward even in this life; the "cup of cold water" we give sometimes returns to refresh our own parched lips. It was some comfort to Lucy, even in this time of sorrow, to feel that she had been enabled to help Nelly to know the Saviour, whom the poor, friendless child seemed to have received into her heart with a true and simple faith.

IX.

INTRODUCTIONS.

"My God, my Father, while I stray
Far from my home in life's rough way,
Oh teach me from my heart to say,
'Thy will be done.'"

THE short January afternoon was closing in, when Lucy's train drew near its destination. Gradually thickening clusters of houses, a momentary glimpse of distant steeples, a general commotion and hunting-up of tickets, packages, and bandboxes, betokened, even to Lucy's inexperienced eyes, that the city was nearly reached.

She had made no acquaintances on the way, but a polite elderly gentleman who had been sitting beside her, and had occasionally exchanged a kind word with her, seeing that she was alone, stopped to hand her out with great courtesy.

"Any one to meet you?" he asked, seeing that she seemed at a loss what to do next.

"Yes—that is—I expect—" faltered Lucy, looking round to see if Stella was not to be seen among the hurrying crowd. But no familiar face was to be seen, and the gentleman who had caught only the first word of her answer, hurried off with a friend he met, forgetting all about Lucy.

It seemed to her a long time that she stood there wistfully watching the people who were meeting their friends, or hurrying away alone; and her spirits, temporarily excited by the journey, began to sink fast. It seemed so strange that no one should be there to meet her, as her uncle had promised; and if no one should appear, what was she to do?

At last, after about five minutes had elapsed, a slight, delicate-looking young man, very fashionably dressed, with an eye-glass at one eye and a cigar in his mouth, sauntered along, lightly swinging his cane and looking leisurely around him. Presently he came up to Lucy, and after a scrutinizing glance, he said, touching his hat:

"My cousin, Lucy Raymond, I presume?" and seeing he was right, he added, with a nonchalant air, "Glad to see you; been waiting long?"

"About a quarter of an hour," Lucy replied, thinking she was speaking the exact truth.

"Hardly that," he replied; "I expected to have been here in time, but these trains are never to be depended on."

Then he motioned to a cabman, who advanced and asked for the checks for the luggage.

Lucy had forgotten all about them, and her cousin mentally set her down as "green," while she nervously searched for them.

"Take your time," he said, good-humoredly.

They were found at last, and everything being collected, Lucy and her cousin were soon driving away from the station.

"You are cousin Edwin, I suppose," Lucy ventured to say timidly.

"The same, at your service. I suppose Stella posted you up about us all? You've

INTRODUCTIONS.

never been in a place as big as this, have you?" he said, observing her eager, watching look.

"No, never; Ashleigh is hardly more than a village. How is Stella?"

"Stella? Oh she's quite well; she was out walking when I left."

Lucy's heart sank at the apparent coldness of her reception. Had Stella been coming to visit *her*, she would have been watching for the steamboat for an hour before its arrival!

"Left all well at home?" inquired Edwin. "Oh, I forgot; I suppose you're all broken up there now?" he added, glancing at her black dress and crape veil. "Fred's gone to college again, I suppose."

"Yes," replied Lucy; she could not have added a word more. It was all she could do to keep back the tears that started to her eyes, as the sad realization that she had no longer a home came back to her. Edwin, however, had happily exhausted his stock of conversation for the present, and Lucy did not try to renew it.

After driving, as it seemed to her, an interminably long way, they stopped opposite a tall stone house, one of a row all just alike, and looking very monotonous and sombre to Lucy's eyes, accustomed to the variety of the Ashleigh houses.

Light gleamed already through the hall-door, which was speedily opened, and the next moment Stella, looking as pretty as ever, rushed down the wide staircase, and met her cousin with an affectionate embrace.

"Mamma, here's Lucy," she said as she led the way up the staircase. At its head stood a lady, who reminded Lucy strongly of the pictures of her dear mother, except that there was the difference of expression between a worldly and an unworldly character. Mrs. Brooke never had had—perhaps now never could have—the pure spiritual beauty which had been Mrs. Raymond's chief charm. But she was a graceful, stylish-looking woman, rather languid and unenergetic in appearance, as she was in character. Her kiss was affectionate as she told Lucy that she was very glad to see her, and that she reminded her a little of her poor mother; "though you're much more like your papa," she added.

"And here are Ada and Sophy, just in time," exclaimed Stella, as two young ladies, very fashionably attired in walking-dress, ascended the stairs, and were duly introduced. Ada, who was the smaller of the two, resembled her mother and Stella, with all their softness and winning grace of manner. Sophy was a tall, handsome girl, with a somewhat haughty air, and her greeting was colder and more dignified. She suggested that Stella should take her cousin at once to her room, saying she should think Lucy would wish to rest for a while before dinner; a proposal to which she was only too glad to accede, feeling somewhat uncomfortable in the heavy travelling attire which was such a contrast to her cousins' elegant dresses.

Stella led the way to a room much larger and more handsomely furnished than Lucy's old one at home, though it all looked so strange and unfamiliar that she wondered whether it would ever seem home to her. Stella showed her all its conveniences and all dear home friends and familiar surroundings, she might be helped to love those around her now, and to do her duty in her new circumstances.

Her heart was much lighter and calmer now, and she was nearly ready to go down to dinner, when Stella came in to help her and to insist on arranging her hair in a new fashion she had lately learned, before escorting her down to the dining-room. Lucy had dreaded a good deal her introduction to her uncle, of whom she had not a very pleasant impression. He was a brisk, shrewd-looking man, a great contrast to his listless-looking son; and his manner, though patronizing, was not ungenial, as Lucy had feared it would be, from his harsh opinions, quoted by Stella, in regard to the poor. All the rest of the family she had already seen, Edwin being the only son who had survived, and on that account probably, a good deal spoilt.

Lucy could not help noticing the very slight mourning worn by the family, if, indeed, it could be called mourning at all. But even this slight mark of respect would hardly have

INTRODUCTIONS.   155

been accorded to Mr. Raymond's memory, but for Lucy's coming among them in her deep mourning. "People would notice, and it wouldn't look well," Sophy had said, and this decided the question, though the girls grumbled a good deal at the inconvenience of it, especially at a time of the year when they were usually so gay, and wanted to wear colors. Stella was the only one who did not object. She had imbibed a strong respect for her uncle, and wore her black dress with a certain satisfaction, in the feeling that she was doing honor to his memory.

There was a good deal of lively talk during dinner, almost unintelligible, however, to Lucy, from her ignorance of the persons and things talked about. The tone of conversation, however, was as uncongenial as were the subjects. Edwin had a cynical air, partly real, partly affected, and the girls' remarks were characterized by the same sort of flippancy which had often jarred upon her in Stella.

After dinner Edwin disappeared, Mr. Brooke became absorbed in his newspapers, Sophy was soon engrossed with a novel, and Ada and her mother employed themselves in some very pretty worsted embroidery. Lucy of course had no work as yet, and Stella resorted to her old fashion of lounging about, doing nothing in particular, except talking. She expatiated largely, for Lucy's benefit, upon the classes and masters in the fashionable school to which her cousin was to accompany her, giving her various scraps of information respecting her future class-mates, with a list of their foibles and peculiarities amusingly described, but rather wearisome to a stranger. Mrs. Brooke questioned Lucy about her previous studies, looking doubtful when she heard of Latin and mathematics, and saying she was afraid "she had been made a little of a blue." At her aunt's request she sat down at the handsome piano, and rather nervously got through a simple air, the only one she knew by heart. She felt she had not done herself justice, and Stella said apologetically, "You know she never had any teacher but Mrs. Steele, and she has no style."

Lucy's cheek flushed at the disparaging remark, but Mrs. Brooke only said: "I hope

INTRODUCTIONS. 157

you will play better than that, my dear, when you have had Signor Goldoni for awhile. Do you sing?"

"Only hymns, aunt. We often sing them on Sundays at home."

"Well, if you have anything of a voice, you will soon do better than that. Any one can sing hymns."

Lucy made no reply, but she privately thought that very few could sing them like her aunt Mary. Then recollecting that Stella had told her how well Sophy played and sang, she turned rather timidly to her with the request, "Won't you sing, cousin Sophy?"

"Do, Sophy," added her mother and Stella, both at once.

But Sophy, reclining in a luxurious easy-chair near the fire, and absorbed in a sensational novel, was too comfortable to think of moving.

"I really can't just now," she said rather coldly. "I'm tired, and I'm just at the most interesting place in this book."

"Sophy never will sing to please any one but herself, and —— *some* people," said Stella mischievously. "And then, sometimes, if she takes the notion, there's no stopping her. Now, if a certain person I know were here—"

Ada laughed; Sophy just said haughtily, "I'll be much obliged to you, Stella, not to disturb me;" at which Stella, with mock gravity, put her finger on her lip.

"Well, I am tired," Mrs. Brooke at last said, rising, "and I am sure Lucy must be so too. Lucy, I advise you to go to bed at once; and Stella, don't stay in your cousin's room, talking; and don't wake Amy, if she is asleep."

It seemed very strange to Lucy that the family circle should break up for the night, without the united acknowledgment of the protecting kindness which had carried them in safety through the day, without invoking the same protecting care through the watches of the night, without the acknowledgment of the sins of the day, and the prayer for forgiveness and the petitions for dear absent ones, to which she had always been accustomed. It was plain that no custom of the kind existed in Mr. Brooke's family.

INTRODUCTIONS.

Notwithstanding her mother's prohibition, Stella did linger long in Lucy's room, chattering about one thing after another, Amy's wide-open eyes watching them from her pillow. "I'm going just in a minute," she would say, when Lucy reminded her of what her mother had said, and then she would rush into some new subject. Lucy was tired, and was longing to have a little quiet time to herself, but Stella, who was undressing beside her, and would be in bed and asleep as soon as she should go back to her own room, did not consider that.

"There's Stella, chattering away yet," said Ada, as she and Sophy came up stairs. "Stella, how naughty of you to stay here so long, keeping Lucy up."

"I was just talking about two or three things," said Stella.

"I have no doubt of that," Sophy remarked; "but I'm sure Lucy would prefer to have the conversation postponed till to-morrow."

Ada was examining the various little possessions of Lucy's, which were already on the dressing-table. "Well, if she hasn't got her

Bible out already!" she exclaimed. "What a good child it is. Does it read it every night?"

"I thought every one did," said Lucy, simply, though her cheek flushed at the tone of the remark.

Ada laughed, and Sophy smiled satirically, though she did not speak.

"Well, you are a simple little thing," said Ada. "When you've lived in town for awhile you'll know better."

"Oh, they're all such good people in Ashleigh. I never knew I did so many wicked things till I was there," said Stella.

Lucy looked pained, and Sophy interposed. "Well, you've shocked Lucy enough for one night, and it's high time she, and you, too, were in bed. So come at once, Stella."

Ada and Stella kissed Lucy affectionately, as they followed Sophy out of the room, and Lucy was left alone to think with surprise and distress of the total want of religious feeling which her cousins' remarks betrayed. When she had once more thanked God for his goodness, and implored his supporting help, and had read a few comforting verses out of her Bible, she did not forget to pray that her cousins, who so little appreciated its treasures of divine counsel and consolation, might yet be led to know them for themselves. But the fatigue and excitement of the day had thoroughly tired her out, and almost as soon as her head sank on the pillow, she was fast asleep, dreaming of the happy times past, and the dear friends now so far away.

X.

NEW EXPERIENCES.

"I need Thy presence every passing hour;
Who but Thyself can foil the tempter's power?
When other helpers fail, and comforts flee,
Help of the helpless, Lord, abide with me!"

LUCY could hardly understand where she was, when she awoke the next morning. She had scarcely ever been absent from home in her life; and the strange and unfamiliar aspect of everything around her quite bewildered her, till little Amy's gentle touch recalled the events of the preceding day. Her home-sickness returned for a time; but the strength came for which she prayed, and she was able to go down to breakfast with a cheerful face.

Sophy and her father were the only ones

who appeared at the nominal breakfast hour. Stella had always been late for breakfast at Ashleigh, in summer, so it was not surprising that in winter she should be one of the last to appear. But it did not apparently matter much, for the different members of the family seemed to come to the breakfast-table just as it suited them, and the meal could scarcely be called a social one. Neither Sophy nor her father talked much, he having his newspaper open before him. Lucy was too shy, as yet, to talk, without encouragement, which Sophy did not give, and she felt it a relief when Stella, with her unfailing loquacity, made her appearance.

"You see, it's Saturday morning, so one can have a little more sleep," she said, yawning, as if she had not had enough yet.

"Then why don't you go to bed sooner at night, my dear, if you want more sleep?" asked her father.

But Stella quickly turned the conversation to another subject, and kept up a full stream of talk till Mrs. Brooke and Ada appeared, and soon afterwards Edwin sauntered in.

"Lucy," said her aunt, as she left the breakfast table, "you must let me see your dresses this morning. I am sure you'll want some new things, and you must get them at once!"

"Aunt Mary thought I had all I should want for the winter," said Lucy coloring, for it was a point on which she was sensitive; not wishing, herself, to spend any more on her dress than was absolutely necessary, and desiring, if possible, not to increase her uncle's expenditure on her account.

"Well, we shall see," said Mrs. Brooke, "but you know you cannot dress here exactly as you did at Ashleigh, and I want you to look as well as your cousins."

Lucy felt rather dismayed at the idea of being expected to wear such stylish attire; and she could have cried, as one after another of the articles on which she and Mrs. Steele had bestowed so much pains was pronounced by Mrs. Brooke and Ada "quite out of date" and "not fit to be seen."

Mrs. Brooke, apart from her really kind intentions towards her sister's orphan daughter, was determined that Lucy, who was to be

Stella's constant companion, should not, by shabby or old-fashioned dress, disgrace the family in the eyes of her critical fashionable associates. So it was determined, without reference to Lucy, that Ada and Sophy should take her out forthwith on a shopping excursion, to provide her with what Mrs. Brooke considered essential for her creditable appearance as a member of her family.

After her first uncomfortable feeling had worn off, Lucy really enjoyed her expedition; everything—the busy streets, the crowded buildings, the rattling carts and carriages; above all, the gayly decorated shop-windows—having so much of the charm of novelty for a country girl. The windows of the print-shops and bookstores in particular, she thought so attractive that she wondered how the hurrying passers-by could go on their way without even a glance at their treasures.

The shopping was easily accomplished under Ada's experienced superintendence, and might have been accomplished much more quickly, Lucy thought, had it not been that her cousins would spend so much time in looking over articles which they had no intention of buying, thereby, she thought, putting the obliging shopmen to an immense deal of trouble, and sadly wasting their own morning. But neither of her companions had much sense of the value of time, having no higher aim in living than that of passing it as pleasantly as possible.

At last the important business was concluded, just in time for them to get home for lunch. Lucy felt very tired after her unwonted expedition over the hard city streets, with their bewildering noise and confusion, and was glad to get away as soon as possible to rest. She soon fell asleep, and when she awoke she found Amy sitting quietly beside her, playing with her doll.

"Wont you look at my doll, cousin Lucy," she said. "I got her on my birthday. Her name is Lucy, after *you*."

"After *me?*" said Lucy, surprised. "Did you call her after me before I came?"

"Yes," replied Amy timidly, "for Stella said you were nice and I should love you."

"I hope you will, dear," said Lucy, touched

and gratified, and she kissed her little cousin affectionately, looking pityingly at the pale, delicate face and fragile form. She had always wished to have a little sister of her own, and her heart was quite disposed to take the little girl into a sister's place. She drew her closer, and after talking a little about the doll, she said:

"Does Amy love the good, kind Saviour, who came to die for her?"

The child looked up with a puzzled expression.

"Jesus, you know," added Lucy, thinking that name might be more familiar.

"That is Jesus that my hymn is about. Nurse taught me, 'Gentle Jesus, meek and mild.'"

"Yes. Well, don't you love him, Amy? He loves you very much."

"Does he love me?" asked Amy. "How do you know?"

"Because he says so."

"But he is up in heaven; nurse said my little brother is up there with him."

It was always "nurse." Amy did not seem

to owe much knowledge of that kind to any one else. Lucy tried to explain as simply as possible that, although the Saviour is in heaven, he is as really near us as when he was on earth; and that we have still in the Bible the very words that he spoke while yet among men.

"Are they in there?" asked Amy, looking at Lucy's Bible.

"Yes, dear; you can't read yet, I suppose?"

"Oh no! The doctor says I mustn't learn for a long while."

"Then I will read to you some of the things that Jesus said; would you like that?"

"Oh yes!" said Amy, and Lucy read the account of our Saviour blessing the little children. She was pleased and surprised at the quiet attention and deep interest with which Amy listened, and mentally resolved to try to lead her to know more of that blessed Saviour, of whom as yet she knew so little. Here was some work provided for her already, she thought, and the feeling made her happier than she had been since she left home.

The evening passed away much as the former one had gone, except that it was varied by the presence of visitors, among whom was a gentleman who, Stella privately informed her cousin, was an "admirer" of Sophy's.

"But it's no use, if he knew it, for you know she's engaged already to Mr. Langton. He's such a handsome, nice fellow, and has a large plantation in the South, where he lives. I know she's as fond of him as she can be, though she doesn't like people to think so. Look, now, how she sings for Mr. Austin. I'm afraid he'll think she likes him."

Sophy was by no means indifferent to any admiration, though she was, as Stella had said, very much attached to her betrothed; and it did not quite coincide with Lucy's ideas of love and lovers, founded, it must be confessed, chiefly on books, to observe the seeming pleasure and animation with which Sophy received the attentions and compliments of this young man, whose partiality for her was so plain.

"Surely, it's very wrong in her if she deceives him, and lets him go on liking her," thought Lucy, who, having never before seen an instance of coquetry, did not know how venial many girls who might know better consider the sin of trifling with an affection which must, if encouraged, end in bitter disappointment.

Next day was Sunday, the day always associated in Lucy's mind with the happiest and holiest feelings of the week. In Mr. Raymond's household, even the most careless sojourner could see that the day seemed pervaded by an atmosphere of holy and peaceful rest from the secular cares and occupations unavoidable on other days. All thoughts about these were, as far as possible, laid aside. No arbitrary rules were enforced, but it was plainly Mr. Raymond's earnest desire that the day should be devoted especially to growing in the knowledge of the Lord, and should be considered as sacred to Him who had set it apart. And by providing pleasant and varied occupation suitable for the day, and cultivating a spirit of Christian cheerfulness, he succeeded in making his family feel it no hardship to carry out his wishes. Fred and Lucy, indeed, had learned to love the Lord's day, and to appreciate the privileges it brings with it. But in Mr. Brooke's family it was decidedly a dull day; a day which must be respectably observed, and therefore not available for ordinary purposes; but a day to be got through as easily as possible, shortened at both ends by late rising and unusually early retiring, as well as by naps indulged in during the day, when even the so-called Sunday reading proved somnolent in its tendency. The necessary abstinence from ordinary occupations was partly made up by the freedom with which the conversation was permitted to run loose in secular matters, amusements, gossip, criticisms on dress and conduct, most prejudicial to any good influence that might have been derived from the public exercises of the day, as well as deteriorating to the whole tone of the mind at any time. No wonder, then, that divine truth, heard at church, fell on inattentive ears, and failed to penetrate hearts filled up with the "lusts of other things!" Through a medium so unyielding, how could the soft dew of holy, spiritual influence descend upon the heart, to nourish and fertilize it?

Lucy was down at the usual breakfast-time, but had to wait more than an hour before any one appeared, except Amy, who sat contentedly on her knee and listened to more reading out of Lucy's Testament, and had even learned two verses of a hymn, before Stella at last appeared.

"How foolish you were to get up so early," she said, when Amy had told her how long they had been down. "I think it is so nice to lie as long as you like, Sunday mornings! I used to think it so hard at Ashleigh that you *would* always have breakfast as early as other days!"

"We never saw any reason for being later on Sunday. Indeed, papa always liked to have us earlier. He said it was the most precious day of the week, and that though he could excuse a hard-worked laboring man for taking an extra sleep on Sunday, we had no such excuse; and to try to shorten the day was dishonoring to Him who gave it."

"What in the world would he have said of Edwin then," said Stella, "who often sleeps till it is too late to go to church, and then he stays at home and sleeps more?"

Lucy could not help smiling, but as Sophy came in just then, she did not need to make any reply. Amy was eager to repeat to her sister the hymn she had just been learning, but Sophy did not seem to care about it, and said to Lucy, "You had better not teach her any more hymns. The doctor says she should not be allowed to study anything till her constitution is stronger. Besides, I do n't believe in filling children's heads with things that make them think about death too soon."

Lucy felt a little vexed and a good deal surprised at what was to her so new an experience. She had not dreamed that any one could object to teaching a child those blessed gospel truths which will shed either on life or on death the truest light. But while she felt a strong interest in and attraction towards her cousin Sophy, she instinctively felt that on such subjects she would be quite unapproachable.

Mrs. Brooke surprised Lucy with the unexpected decision that her deficiencies in dress must keep her at home that day. She felt as if it was almost wrong to submit; her dear father would have so much disapproved of any one's staying away from the house of God for such a reason. But then she remembered that while under her aunt's charge, it was her duty to yield a deference to her wishes, unless she absolutely violated her conscience in so doing; and that her father would also have said, "Ye younger, be subject to the elder," and would have told her that, though prevented from going up to an earthly sanctuary, she could worship God at home in the sanctuary of her heart.

But she did not find this so easy, as Stella, glad of the excuse, insisted on staying at home "to keep Lucy company," though Lucy tried to make her understand that she was not desirous of having any "company" while the rest were at church. In vain she tried to fix her attention on her open Bible. Stella would continually break in with some remark which, when answered, was sure to lead to another; and though Lucy's remonstrances at length became somewhat impatient in their tone, it was evidently hopeless to try to reduce her to silence. She, however, at last succeeded in persuading her to listen while she read to Amy, first one or two Bible stories, such as she thought would interest her most, and then a simple story out of one of her own Sunday books which she had brought with her. The earnestness with which Amy drank in every word was a great contrast to Stella's desultory way of listening; but even *she* seemed a little interested in Lucy's reading, and the morning did not seem altogether thrown away.

But in the afternoon Lucy found that trying to read in the drawing-room was quite out of the question, her attention being perpetually distracted by the frivolous conversation almost continually going on there. First one topic was started and then another, and in spite of her efforts to the contrary, she would find herself listening to the gossiping talk going on around her. At last she took refuge in her own room to read there in quiet, though she was before long followed thither by Stella.

"Don't you think, Stella, I might go to church this evening? I don't like staying at home all day, and no one would notice what I had on, I'm sure?" she asked her cousin.

Stella opened her eyes. "Do you mean to say you really want to go?" she asked. "I thought people only went to church because it was a duty."

"I used to go for that reason," Lucy replied, "but I should be sorry if I only went on that account now."

"But why? What pleasure can you find in it? The service always seems to me so long, and the sermon so dry, that it makes me yawn so; I can't help it."

Lucy hesitated a little before answering; it was not easy to explain. "There are many things that make it pleasant. One always hears something to do one good; often the very thing one needs at the very time. It always makes troubles seem lighter and another world more real and near. I always feel so much nearer papa when I am in church," she added, in a lower tone.

"Oh! that is because you always used to hear him preach, I suppose," said Stella, not able to comprehend any other reason. "Well, since you like it so much, I'll ask mamma if if you can't go; but I don't know whether any of the rest are going."

Mrs. Brooke, though as much surprised as Stella at Lucy's strong wish, felt that it ought to be respected. She suggested that instead of going to the large fashionable church which the family usually attended, they should go to a small one in the neighborhood, their usual resort on stormy days. Edwin having got tired of the novel he had been yawning over, good-naturedly offered to be her guide and escort, and Stella made no objection, when her mother told her she had better go too, as she had not been out in the morning.

The stars were twinkling brilliantly through the clear frosty atmosphere, and the long vistas of gas-lamps, seen on all sides, were a novelty to Lucy's country eyes. The streets were full of people, encountering each other as they vended their way to church in opposite directions. There were others, too, not going to church, but to very different places of resort. But of these, Lucy happily knew nothing.

The first hymn was already being sung when they entered the church, a small, plain building. Lucy was at once interested by the thoughtful, earnest face of the clergyman, who reminded her a little of her father. The first prayer, so simple, yet so full of petitions for the things she most needed, carried her heart with it, till she forgot she was not at home still. The text read was, "A very present help in trouble," and the sermon was what might have been expected from the tone of the preceding prayer. It was so full of Christ, pointing to his constant presence, to him as the only true comforter and sustainer, either in sorrow and temptation, that simple as was the language and unpretentious the style, it touched the deepest springs in Lucy's heart, and she leaned back in her seat to hide the soothing, happy tears.

Edwin, however, from his end of the pew, could see that she was crying, and began, out of curiosity, to listen to the sermon to find out what it was that affected her so much. At first he thought it very odd that she should have been so moved by it. But gradually, as he listened to the earnest words in which the preacher, speaking evidently from his own heart, dwelt upon all that Christ might be to the weary soul which had tried earthly pleasures and found them wanting, earthly cisterns and found them broken, a fountain of refreshing, giving strength and energy for the journey of life, the "shadow of a great rock in a weary land," giving to the weary wayfarer rest and shelter from the burden and heat of the day, he began to feel, in spite of his indifference, that there might be a nobler, happier ideal of life than that of seeking to fill the hours as they passed with every variety of pleasure within reach. But it was only a passing thought. Old habits of thinking, so long indulged, came back to fill up his mind as soon as the voice of the speaker had ceased. His plan of life was not likely to be altered yet.

Lucy walked very silently home, watching the starlight trembling through the crystal air, and wondering in what remote, inconceivable sphere are passed those beloved existences which are lost to us here. And then came the happy thought, that though they seem so remote and inaccessible, the Saviour is near at once to them and to those who are left below, and that in communion with him there may be a point of contact, intangible, it is true, but none the less real. Edwin, as he languidly wondered what his quiet cousin was thinking about, did not know that there was a distance immeasurable between his thoughts and hers.

Next day Lucy accompanied her cousin to school, that she might be at once introduced to her new classes and studies. When her acquirements had been duly tested, she found that, while in some superficial accomplishments she was considerably behind Stella, yet in other studies, more solid in their nature, and requiring greater accuracy and deeper thought, she was far in advance of her cousin. This might have considerably increased the tendency she already had to a sense of her own superiority, had it not been that the things in which she was deficient were precisely those which were of most consequence at Mrs. Wilmot's establishment, being more showy, and therefore more easily appreciated.

Her love of approbation made her very anxious to excel in what was valued by those around her, and in her desire to make up lost ground, she happily escaped an undue sense of superiority in what was most valuable, a proficiency which was the result, chiefly, of her father's care.

Fond of study for its own sake, she entered on her class-work with all the zest of one who had never known school-life before, and who was determined to make the most of her opportunities. And her enjoyment of her studies and the stimulus of contest to a great extent counteracted the uncongeniality of her new home, as well as the homesick feeling which came over her when a letter from Mrs. Steele or Fred revived old and happy associations.

XI.

A START IN LIFE.

"His path in life was lowly,
He was a working man;
Who knows the poor man's trials
So well as Jesus can?"

AT Mill-Bank Farm things were going on much as when Nelly Connor had become an inmate there. Under the influence of her watchword Bessie was making good headway against her faults of idleness and carelessness, and her mother declared she was growing a "real comfort" to her. Under her teaching Nelly's reading had progressed so well that she could spell out very creditably a chapter in the New Testament. Jenny and Jack had also been taught their letters, and though they were not to go to Sunday-school

A START IN LIFE.

till the spring, they had already learned from Bessie a good deal of Bible knowledge. Sam was not nearly so often a truant, now that he knew his mother's watchful eye was ready to discover any omission in attending Sunday-school, and the boys were gradually growing in respect for things on which they could see their mother now placed so much importance.

Nelly had never before known so much of comfort and happiness. She was treated as one of the family, and the easy tasks which fell to her lot were labors of love and gratitude. Even the irksome sewing, by dint of patiently struggling with her constitutional restlessness, was growing almost a pleasure, from her being able to do it so much better. In the letters which Bessie occasionally received from Lucy, there was always a kind message for Nelly, which would act as a wonderful stimulus for days after it came.

As the winter wore on, however, it was evident she was not greatly needed by her kind friends. Bessie was growing stronger every day, and more able to assist her mother, and Nelly could not help feeling that she was kept only because she needed a home. One day, therefore, she asked Mrs. Ford if she thought she was not now fit to take a place.

"Well, you've got to be a good little worker, that's a fact; but there's no hurry about your going. You're welcome to stay here as long as you like."

"It's very kind of you, ma'am; but perhaps if you'd be looking out you might hear of some one that would take me, and give me whatever I was worth," said Nelly, in whom the instinct of independence was strong.

A few days after this Mrs. Ford was asked by her friend Mrs. Thompson, what she was going to do with her little Irish girl. "She is big enough for a place," she said, "and there is no good in having a girl like that learning idle ways. I think I know of a place that would suit her very well."

"What place is that?" asked Mrs. Ford.

Mrs. Thompson replied that a friend of hers in the city had written to inquire for a country-girl about Nelly's age. She would have no hard work, and would get such clothing as she required, instead of wages in money.

"You see, servants are very hard to obtain in those large places," remarked Mrs. Thompson, "and they always want the highest wages; and this person is n't very well off, and keeps boarders to support herself, so she can't afford a great deal."

"But would she be good to Nelly?" inquired Mrs. Ford.

Mrs. Thompson promised to inquire of the friend who had written to her, in regard to this point. Her correspondent's reply was tolerably satisfactory. Mrs. Williams, the person who wanted Nelly, was likely to do whatever was right by any girl who might be sent her, as she was a very respectable person, and "a church member." This last statement weighed considerably with Mrs. Ford, and decided her to mention the place to Nelly.

Nelly could not help feeling a throb of regret at hearing that there really was a place open to her, for she dreaded exceedingly the prospect of leaving her kind friends. But of this she said nothing, and tried to seem pleased with the idea of trying the place. One great inducement it certainly had: that it was in the city in which Lucy now resided. She hoped to see Miss Lucy sometimes, and she would help her to be good and do well, she thought. Mrs. Ford also thought this circumstance a favorable one, as Lucy could see for herself whether Nelly was comfortably situated, and if not, could help her to find a better place. So after much consideration and some misgivings, it was reluctantly settled that she should go. Mrs. Thompson's brother was going to the city soon, and Nelly could accompany him.

She did not need a great deal of time for preparation, though Mrs. Ford kindly provided her with all that was necessary for her respectable appearance in her new place: so that she went back to the city which had been her former abode, a very different looking girl from the bare-footed, gypsy-like child who had wandered, uncared for, about its streets. "I know the place well, ma'am," she said to Mrs. Ford; "it isn't as if I had never been there; I wont feel a bit strange;" and though the spring was approaching, and she was for many reasons very sorry to leave Ashleigh, she did not dread the thought of going to the great city, alone and friendless, as much as a thoroughly country-bred girl would have done.

When her travelling companion bade her good-by at the railway station, Nelly, not in the least frightened by the hurrying crowds and the noisy streets, so familiar to her of old, took up her little bundle, containing all the worldly goods she possessed, and set off briskly to look for the address inscribed on the card she held in her hand. She did not need to ask her way more than once, though it was a half hour's walk before she reached the street, and then she walked slowly along studying the numbers of the doors, till she arrived at the right one, bearing on a brass plate the words, "Mrs. Williams' Boarding-House." It was one of the most bare and uninviting of a dull row, and not even the bright sunshine of the early spring could enliven it much. Other houses had flowers or birds in the windows, or at least pleasant glimpses of white curtains; but this one, with its half-closed blinds, had almost a funereal aspect. Nelly had a keen susceptibility of externals, and her heart sank a little; but she rang the bell, determined to make the best of it. The door was opened by an elderly woman in rusty black, with a hard, careworn face, which did not relax into the slightest perceptible smile, as she regarded Nelly scrutinizingly, saying at last, "Oh, you're the girl Mrs. Thompson was to send, I suppose."

"Yes, ma'am," replied Nelly, who had not yet been invited to enter.

"Well, you're not as big as I thought you'd be, and you don't look very strong. Come in;" and she led the way into a dull, bare dining-room, where she went on with her work of setting the table, while she put Nelly through an examination as to her qualifications. She either was, or appeared to be, dissatisfied, and after dryly expressing a hope that she would suit, she told her to follow her down to the kitchen.

It was a dark, cellar-like place, with an equally cellar-like room of very small dimensions opening off it, where Nelly was to sleep. Many houses seem built on the principle—not the Christian one of loving our neighbors as ourselves—that "anything is good enough for servants." As if light, and air, and pleasant things to look out upon, were not just as much needed by them as by their employers. Kitchens and servants' rooms need not be luxurious. It would be doing servants an injury to accustom them to luxuries, of which they would sometime feel the privation; but many of them have been accustomed to pure, free air, and a pleasant outlook, and feel the reverse far more than is imagined by those who condemn them to live in under-ground cells.

Nelly felt her abode very dismal, after the light, airy farm-house; even from her old attic-window she had a pleasant view of the river, and could always see the moon and stars at night; while from this, the utmost she could see from the windows was a little bit of street pavement. But when she unpacked her bundle, and came upon her "watchword card," as Lucy had called it, her courage rose as she remembered that her heavenly Friend was as near her here as in the free, fresh country; and that where he was, he could make it home. She could not have put this feeling into words, but it was there, in her heart, where doubtless he himself had put it.

It was some time before Mrs. Williams thought of inquiring whether she had had any dinner. On her replying in the negative—she was beginning to feel quite tired and faint—Mrs. Williams, with a half-reluctant air, brought out of a locked cupboard some very dry-looking bread, and cold meat, which she set before Nelly.

She was very hungry, so that even this was very acceptable, and she did justice to the meal. Before she had finished, a voice called from an upper story, "Mother, tell the new girl to bring up some water."

Nelly was accordingly directed to fill the water-can and take it up to the top of the house. After carrying it up three flights of stairs, she saw a door open, and a girl of nineteen or twenty, apparently engaged in performing an elaborate toilet, looked out from it.

"How old are you?" she said, as she took the water from Nelly.

"I'll soon be fourteen, miss."

"Well, you do n't look it. You'll have to look sharp here if you want to suit us. Now take these boots down to brush."

She spoke in a quick, sharp way, a good deal like her mother's; and her face, though tolerably comely, was sharp, too. Miss Williams meant to "get on" in the world, if she could, and her face and manner showed it.

Nelly found various things to do before she got back to her unfinished dinner, and then Mrs. Williams hurried her through, that she might get the kitchen made "tidy." In the meantime Miss Williams departed, in all the glories of a fashionable toilette, for her afternoon promenade, her mother regarding her with much pride and complacency. It seemed the one object of her hard-working, careworn life, that her daughter should look "like a lady," and a large proportion of her earnings and savings went to effect this object.

Nelly's services were at once called into requisition to assist in the preparation of the dinner for the boarders—four gentlemen—who, her mistress informed her, were "very particular," and liked everything nice. She received a confusing multiplicity of directions as to waiting at table, for Mrs. Williams rather prided herself on the "stylishness" of her establishment. She got through her task tolerably well, though somewhat bewildered between Mrs. Williams' quick, sharp reminders and the "chaffing" of one or two of the gentlemen, who thought it "good fun" to puzzle the "new hand" with ironical remarks, some of them being aimed at their landlady through her servant.

After the waiting at dinner, followed the preparation of tea for Mrs. Williams and her daughter, who had come in, and was in the midst of one of the evening performances on the piano which were the dread of the boarders; and then there were all the dishes used at dinner to wash and put away. It was pretty late by the time all this had been done, and Nelly was feeling very sleepy, and wondering how soon she might go to bed, when her mistress came down with half a dozen pairs of boots, to be cleaned either that evening or next morning. Now the next day was Sunday, and at the farm, Mrs. Ford had of late insisted on the excellent rule of getting all done that could be done on Saturday night, so as to leave the Lord's day as free as possible from secular duties. So Nelly, sleepy as she was, took up her blacking brushes, and proceeded to rub and polish with all her might. But fatigue was too strong for her, and before she had got through the third pair her head sank down and she lost all consciousness, till she suddenly started up, thinking Mrs. Ford was calling her to drive the cows to pasture. It was impossible to rouse herself again to her work; she just managed to put out her light, and hastily undressing, she threw herself on the bed with only a half-conscious attempt at her usual evening prayer, which, however, He who knows the weakness of our frame would surely accept.

Next morning she started up instantly at Mrs. Williams' impatient call. She could hardly get ready quick enough to satisfy her mistress, and had no time to kneel down and ask her heavenly Father's help for the duties of the day. Mrs. Williams had not thought of this need for herself, and still less for her little handmaid. . She found there was plenty of work before her, independently of the boots that remained to be cleaned. By the time she had got through, the bells were ringing for church, and it was time to think of getting the dinner ready, the boarders dining early on Sunday. Mrs. Williams was not going to church herself. The gentlemen always expected the dinner to be especially good on that day, without much consideration what the cook's Sunday might be; and it was much too important a matter to be left to Nelly's inexperienced hands. But during the time when her mistress was occupied in helping her daughter to dress her hair elaborately for church, Nelly found a little quiet time to read part of a chapter, and learn a verse, and ask God's help to do right during the day, and to remember that it was his day, the best of all the week.

So prepared, she found the difficult task of performing unaccustomed duties to her mistress' satisfaction, easier than it might otherwise have been. For why should we consider anything too small to seek His aid, by whom

A START IN LIFE. 195

the hairs of our head are all numbered? And the very attitude of trust and reliance on him, calms and clears the mind and strengthens the heart.

There was no time for Nelly to go to church on that Sunday at any rate. She could not get through her work with her comparatively unpractised hands, and it was with a very weary body and mind that she read her evening verse, and repeated her favorite hymn, "I lay my sins on Jesus," as a sort of substitute for her usual Sunday-school lessons, and then lay down to think of the kind friends she had left, and to wonder when she should see Miss Lucy, till she fell asleep to dream that she was at the farm again, and churning butter that would not come.

Bessie had written to Lucy, telling her of Nelly's departure, but had forgotten to give her mistress' address, so that Lucy could not find her out till she should go to see her at Mr. Brooke's. And for many days this was impracticable. Day after day passed, filled with the same unceasing routine of drudgery, and though her growing skill enabled her to get through her work more quickly, this did not add to her leisure, since, as her capabilities increased, her duties increased also. Miss Williams, too, who objected to do anything for herself, when another could be got to do it, found Nelly very convenient for all sorts of personal services.

Nelly went through it all without grumbling, though she often went to bed quite tired out. But youth and health came to her aid, and she would wake in the morning to go singing about her work. She had an uncommonly sweet voice, and the boarders used often to remark to each other that there was more music in her untaught snatches of song than in all Miss Williams' attempts at the piano.

But as weeks went on, the perpetual, unceasing strain began to wear upon her, and her songs grew less and less frequent. Though she was almost too busy to indulge in many longings for Ashleigh and its pleasant fields, it was a little hard to know that the beautiful budding spring was passing into summer, and that she could taste none of the country pleasures she had so much enjoyed last year; that the only sign by which she knew the advancement of the season was the increasing heat, enervating her frame and undermining her strength; its effect in this respect being greatly heightened by the close, heavy atmosphere in which she chiefly lived. Nature is stronger than man, after all, and when the upper classes selfishly neglect the comfort of their poorer brethren, they will find that inexorable nature will avenge the infringement of her laws, and will touch their own interests in so doing.

"I can't think what has come over Nelly," Mrs. Williams would say to her daughter. "She's not the same girl she was when she came here, and she seems to grow lazier every day. Well, it's the way with them all. A new broom sweeps clean."

But Mrs. Williams might easily have found a truer explanation of Nelly's failing energies than this convenient proverb, in the unwholesome atmosphere she was breathing by night and day, as well as in the quantity and quality of the food provided for her. Mrs. Williams would have indignantly repelled the charge of starving Nelly, but she forgot the requirements of a fast-growing girl. Everything eatable was kept rigidly locked up; that was a fundamental principle of Mrs. Williams' housekeeping, and Nelly's allowance was sometimes so scanty, and at other times composed of such an uninviting collection of scraps, that she often had not sufficient nourishment to repair the waste of strength which she was continually undergoing. And as she would rather suffer than ask more, her constitution was really giving way for want of sufficient sustenance.

So two or three months passed, and she had not yet seen Lucy. She had only indeed been two or three times at church, for Mrs. Williams never seemed to remember that her little servant had an immortal soul to be nourished, though it must be admitted that she was not much more mindful of her own spiritual welfare. As for getting out on week-days, except on her mistress' errands, Mrs. Williams seemed to consider that quite out of the question, and, indeed, Nelly could not easily have found leisure for half an hour's absence. One evening at last, when most of the boarders were dining out, Mrs. Williams graciously acceded to Nelly's request to be allowed to go out for an hour; "but don't stay a minute longer," she added. Nelly had carefully kept Lucy's address, and gladly set off, as fast as she could walk, towards the quarter of the city in which she knew it to be. She steered her course pretty straight, but had walked for fully half an hour before she reached the door, on the brass plate of which she read, "B. Brooke."

It was with a beating heart that she put the question, "Is Miss Lucy Raymond at home?" to be answered in the negative by the servant, who inwardly wondered what a girl so poorly dressed could want with Miss Lucy. Waiting was out of the question; she would be late enough in getting back, as it was, so she sorrowfully turned away, without leaving any message. It was a great disappointment, and tired and dispirited she made her way back.

There was another reason, besides want of time, to prevent her making a second attempt. The clothes with which she had been provided on leaving Mill-Bank Farm, were almost worn out with the hard work she had to do, and

Mrs. Williams had as yet done nothing towards fulfilling her promise of giving her necessary clothing, although Nelly's tattered frock was worn beyond all possibility of repairing. Nelly was conscious of the doubtful look with which she was regarded when she asked for Lucy, and she shrank from again encountering it, and perhaps bringing discredit on Miss Lucy in the eyes of her city friends, by her own disreputable appearance.

One afternoon in June—Mrs. Williams and her daughter being out—Nelly having a few minutes to spare, was standing at the open door, listening to the plaintive strains of an organ-grinder who was playing close by. His dark Italian face looked sad and careworn, and the little girl beside him, evidently his daughter from the resemblance between them, looked so pale and feeble that it seemed as if her little thin hands could scarcely support the tambourine she was ringing in accompaniment to a little plaintive song. Nelly enjoyed the performance exceedingly, but her admiration did not appear to be shared by those whose applause was of more consequence, for

A START IN LIFE. 201

not a single penny found its way into the poor man's hat, either from the inmates of the house or from the juvenile bystanders. His discouraged air, and the sad, wistful eyes of the little girl, touched Nelly's warm Irish heart, as he leaned on Mrs. Williams' doorsteps to rest himself while he set down his organ, experience having taught him that it was a useless waste of strength to play before that door.

Nelly, seeing how hot and tired he looked, impulsively asked the poor man whether he would walk in and sit down, never stopping to think whether she had a right to do so. He looked up, surprised at the invitation, but thankfully accepted it, and Nelly brought two chairs into the hall for him and the little girl. Then, as the only entertainment she was able to supply, she filled two glasses with the coldest water she could find, and shyly offered them to her guests.

"Ah, it is good," said the organ-grinder, when he had drained his glass. "Many thanks," he added in his foreign accent; and the little girl looked up into Nelly's face with the sweetest, most expressive grateful smile.

"Now," said the Italian, after having rested a little, "you love music; is it not true? or you would not be so kind to us. I will play for you."

And, taking up his instrument, he played an air sweeter than any Nelly had yet heard from him, and the little girl sang, in her liquid voice, a little song, the words of which she could not understand, for they were Italian.

"Now we must go," said the man. "Good by, my good girl; if I were home, in my country, I would do as much for you." And the father and daughter pursued their weary way, Nelly's eyes following wistfully the forms of those whom she regarded as friends already, for were they not, like herself, poor, lonely strangers in a strange land?

Then she began to wonder whether she had done wrong in asking them to come in. She knew instinctively that she could not have done it had Mrs. Williams been at home. But yet she could not feel such a simple, common act of kindness to have been wrong. No harm had been done to anything belonging to her mistress, and the "cup of cold water," had she not a right to offer it to those who needed it so much?

After that the organ-grinder and his child passed frequently through that street, and whenever she could, Nelly would exchange a few kind words with them, and the man would play for her, knowing well that she had no pennies to offer in return. But at such times she used to wish so much that she had a little money of her own.

The Italian would sometimes look at her tattered dress and her face, gradually growing thinner and paler, as if he thought her quite as forlorn as himself; and once, when he heard her mistress call her in, and scold her for "talking to such characters in the street," he shook his head, and muttered something in his native tongue.

And so it came to pass that the poor Italian and his daughter became Nelly's only friends in that great, busy city.

XII.

AMBITION.

"Tell me the same old story
When you have cause to fear,
That this world's empty glory
Is costing me too dear."

LUCY'S interest in her studies, and the zeal with which she pursued them, had had a wonderful effect in reconciling her to her new circumstances. She could sometimes hardly believe that only a few short months lay between her and her old life, now seeming so far back in the distance. Her progress in study had been very rapid, as her abilities were above the average, and her love of study was much greater than was usual among her companions, most of whom looked upon their school education chiefly as a matter of form,

AMBITION. 205

which it was expected of them to go through before entering on the real object of life, the entrance into "society" with its pleasures and excitements. That it was intended to be a means of disciplining their minds for better doing their future duties, enlarging their range of thought, and opening to them new sources of interest and delight, had never entered into their heads. Lucy, indeed, pursued her studies more for the sake of the pleasure they afforded her at the time, than with any ulterior views, though she did feel the advantages placed in her way to be a sacred trust, and like all other privileges, to be accounted for to Him who had bestowed them.

With her teachers, who found her a pupil after their own heart, she was a much greater favorite than she was with some of her classmates, who were so uncongenial that she could not well enter into, or even understand the things which interested them. Nor could she always refrain from showing her impatience of their frivolities, or her contempt for the follies which so engrossed their minds; and this did not, of course, tend to make her popular. This circumstance Lucy did not care for so much even as she ought, for, though fond of approbation, she cared only for the approbation of those she esteemed, unlike her cousin Stella, who liked admiration from any source.

When the bright balmy days of spring came, bringing with them thoughts of green fields and budding trees, there sometimes came over her longings, almost irresistible, for her old home, so full of rural sights and sounds, in such contrast to the stiff, straight city streets and houses, the dust and noise, and the squares planted with trees, which to her eyes seemed like caged birds, as the only reminders that there were such things in the world. These longings usually came to her most strongly in the long spring evenings, in whose lengthening light she used to rejoice at Ashleigh, as enabling her to prolorg her pleasant country rambles. Now she must either walk up and down the hard pavements between never-ending rows of houses, or sit at the window, wistfully watching the sunset light falling golden on the opposite walls. Now and then she accompanied the others in a long drive; but the distance which they had to traverse before they reached anything like the country, seemed to her interminable; and when they did catch a glimpse of fields and woods, it seemed hard to have so soon to turn back and lose sight of them again.

On her return from one of these drives, which had been protracted till dusk, she was told that she had been inquired for by a girl, very poorly dressed, "almost like a beggar." She was puzzled at first, but almost immediately it flashed across her that it must be Nelly Connor. She had often thought of her since she had come to the city, but could not find her, owing to Bessie's omission to give her mistress' address, an omission which Bessie, not being a good correspondent, and naturally supposing that Nelly would soon find her way to Lucy, had not yet remedied. "Oh, I wish I had seen her," exclaimed Lucy. much to the surprise both of the servants and her cousins, who could not understand how a girl of that description should come to be so interesting to her as to cause so much disappointment at having missed her, and at having no clue to her place of abode.

"I hope she will soon come again," was the reflection with which Lucy consoled herself, and Stella explained to Sophy and Edwin: "It's a little Irish *protégée* of hers that she was crazy about at Ashleigh, and she used to lecture me because I did n't think as much of her as she did." Lucy laughed and tried to explain, but stopped, seeing that her cousins took very little interest in the matter.

Lucy did not come much in contact with her uncle and aunt. The former was much absorbed in business, and though a kind and indulgent parent, especially to his favorite Stella, he interfered but little in home matters. Mrs. Brooke, who had always been a rather negative character, had long given up to her elder daughters any sway she had ever held, and was almost entirely guided by their judgment, of which they naturally took advantage to indulge to the utmost their own love of gayety. Balls and parties in winter, and in summer gay picnics and driving parties without end, engrossed their time and thoughts, to the exclusion of higher objects of interest. Ada was fond of embroidery, and would betake herself to it when nothing better was going on, and Sophy was sometimes persuaded to paint for a fancy sale one of the illuminations, in doing which she evinced great talent. They were generally quotations from the poets, which she selected, and as Lucy watched the taste with which Sophy blended and contrasted the rich coloring, she would long for the same skilful hand, in order to clothe in such glowing colors some of the favorite texts which shone for her like beams of light from heaven.

But she had no talent for drawing, and though by diligent practice she improved very much in playing and singing, she knew she should never be able to do either like her cousin Sophy. How useful, she thought, might she not be, if her heart were but actuated by love to Christ. She felt she dared not speak to her on this subject, but she often prayed to Him who can command the hearts of all, that He would touch and renew that of her cousin Sophy.

Between Stella and Amy, dissimilar as they were, there existed a strong cousinly affection. Stella, with all her bantering ways, would never now go so far as seriously to annoy her, generally taking her side when she thought the others were too much for her. But though Lucy tried earnestly to draw her cousin towards the knowledge of her Saviour; all such attempts seemed to glance off her, like raindrops from an oiled surface. She was quite satisfied with herself as she was, and had not yet found out the insufficiency of the earthly pleasures which at present satisfied her. She believed, of course, in another world, and the need of a preparation for it, but she thought there was plenty of time for that, and it had never entered within the range of her comprehension that the change of heart, which is the necessary preparation for a future life, is as necessary to living either well or happily in the present. So that Lucy was constantly feeling that, in the most important matters of all, there could be no genuine sympathy between them.

Nor among her school-mates was her longing for sympathy between them more fully gratified. They were all actuated by the "spirit of this world which passeth away," and avoided everything that could bring the thought of another to their minds, so that she had not found one with whom she could speak on the subjects most dear to her, or hold an intercourse mutually helpful.

There was, indeed, one of her school-mates, a Miss Eastwood, a boarder at Mrs. Wilmot's, in whom, from her sweet, serious manner and appearance, and from some other tokens, she thought she might have found a congenial friend. But Miss Eastwood was a little older than herself, and Lucy's natural shyness was increased by the impression that she rather avoided her and Stella, probably from knowing that Mr. Brookes' was a thoroughly worldly family, and supposing that Lucy must be like her cousins in this respect. Miss Eastwood, in this, was acting conscientiously, yet such a determined avoidance of those who appear to be worldly in their principles of action, though founded on the desire of keeping out of temptation, sometimes lead to great mistakes. Real Christian sympathy may sometimes be found, where from circumstances there may seem to be least appearance of it, and even where it does not exist, influence for good might be exerted over those whom distrust must necessarily repel. He who sat with publicans and sinners, while He enjoins His followers to be "not of the world," even as He was not of the world, cannot, surely, desire them to avoid all opportunities naturally occurring, of coming in contact with those who may not be like-minded; and if Christians would always show their true colors uncompromisingly, while coming near to others as God's providence opens opportunity, they would both do more good, and find sympathy and fellowship oftener than they expect.

Of all the inmates of her uncle's house, little Amy was the one in whom Lucy found the greatest congeniality. Her readings to her, and her teaching about Jesus, seemed to have satisfied a craving of the child's little heart, and she drank in the truths which Lucy tried to explain to her, with the eagerness of

AMBITION. 213

one who had been thirsting for the living water. Indeed, she needed very little explanation; it seemed as if the Spirit of God was her teacher, instructing her in things that might have seemed too deep for so young a child to grasp. Though, indeed, there may be less difference than we often imagine, between the mind of a child and that of the wisest man as regards their power of comprehending truths that are too infinitely profound for the greatest human intellect to fathom.

Amy had, from her infancy, been so delicate that she had been in a great measure confined to the nursery all her life, and not being nearly so winning and attractive as Stella, she had never been so great a favorite with her brothers and sisters, who, never having taken the trouble of drawing her out, considered her rather uninteresting. The death of a fine little boy, a little older than Amy, had strangely had the effect upon her mother of making her turn away, almost with a feeling of impatience, from the unattractive, ailing child that had been spared, while her noble little boy, so full of beauty and promise, had been taken. Amy had been left almost entirely to her nurse, who had taught her some of the simple prayers and hymns that she herself had learned at Sunday-school, though she had not spoken to her of Jesus, as Lucy had done. The story of his love fell upon a heart that was unconsciously yearning for a fuller measure of affection than it had ever received from human sources, and the love which it excited in return, for Him whom the child seemed at once to recognize as an ever near and present friend, became the most powerful influence of her life. She never wearied of hearing about him, of asking questions about him, particularly about his childhood, which often threw light, in her young teacher's mind, upon things which she had not considered before. The child's intense interest, too, and the simplicity of her childish faith, were no small help to Lucy, in the midst of much that might have drawn her heart and mind away from her first love. For there were many temptations in her way—temptations which sometimes overcame her. Even her zeal in her studies often unduly absorbed her mind, tempting her to leave the fag-end of time and strength for prayer and the reading of God's word, and her natural ambition often led her into unchristian feelings and tempers. Then, when humbled and discouraged, and doubtful whether she really was a child of God at all, some simple, loving remark of Amy's would drive away the clouds, and she would come again, in penitence and faith, to drink of the living water which alone can quench human thirst.

Sometimes the spiritual beauty of her little cousin's expression, and her growing ripeness for a better country, would awaken a feeling of regret that Amy was not more like other children, lest indeed she might be ripening for an early removal. Yet the thought would recur: "Amy is not fit for the roughness of the world; why should I wish her stay upon it, instead of going home to rest in her Saviour's bosom?"

Fred had paid a short visit to his sister, as soon as his college vacation commenced. But he had made an engagement for the summer, as a tutor, and he was obliged to hasten away to his duties, before Lucy had said half of what she wished to say, or asked his advice on half the subjects on which she had been longing for it. However, short as his visit was, it was very useful, as well as very pleasant, reviving old thoughts and habits of feeling which were in danger of falling into the background, and stimulating her to follow the example of a brother who was so steadfastly bent on following his Lord.

As the time for the summer examinations at Mrs. Wilmet's drew near, Lucy, bent on carrying off two or three of the prizes, redoubled her application to her studies. But she allowed her desire to accomplish her object to carry her too far. All her thoughts, all her time, were so engrossed by it, that she had none to spare for anything else. She would not join her cousins in any of their innocent recreations, and became impatient and irritable when she met with claims upon her time that could not be set aside. Even the Lord's day at last began to seem an interruption to the work in which she was so eager. Her too intense application began to affect her health; she was growing so nervous that Stella would sometimes declare that she was changing her identity, and could not be the same Lucy Raymond as of old. Lucy could indeed feel the change in herself, and this only increased the irritation instead of leading her to remove the cause, by moderating the ambition which was leading her to a blamable excess in what would otherwise have been praiseworthy diligence. But just at that time the coveted prizes seemed to throw everything else into the shade, and she had no watchful, judicious friend to point out, in timely warning, the snare into which she was falling.

Even little Amy, for the first time, occasionally found herself impatiently put aside, and her requests to be read to met with, "Not now, Amy; I have n't time! Do n't tease me now, like a good child;" and would steal away with a surprised look in her soft eyes, wondering how it could be that cousin Lucy should not have time to read to her about Jesus.

One of the prizes on which Lucy had most set her heart, was that to be given for History, one of her favorite studies. In ancient and classical history she had been very thoroughly grounded by her father, and had nothing to fear, most of the principal events being familiar to her as household words. But her knowledge of modern history was not so extensive, and she had a great deal of hard study before she could feel at all at ease in competing with her classmates, some of whom were considerably older than herself, and had given most of their attention to modern history, the division in which the greater number of questions were asked.

Lucy had studied with so much diligence, and her daily recitations were always so good, that she had great hopes of taking the first prize, and her master, with whom she was a great favorite, did not conceal his expectation of her success. Just the day before the examination, when looking over the list of subjects for revision, she found, to her dismay, that she had unaccountably overlooked one of those prescribed. It was quite too late to hope to repair the omission satisfactorily, but she hastily procured the proper book, and set to work, at once, to try to gain such a general knowledge of the subject as would enable her to reply to the questions that were certain to be asked upon it. But her overtasked mind refused to grasp the words that swam before her eyes, and a headache, which had been annoying her for days, became so severe that she was obliged to shut the book and throw herself on the bed, her oppressed mind relieving itself in a burst of tears.

While she was still crying, Amy came in, and going up to her, stroked her cheek with her loving little hands. "Are you hurt, cousin Lucy?" she asked wonderingly; and as her cousin shook her head, she asked in a lower tone, "Were you naughty, cousin Lucy?" these being to her the only conceivable causes for sorrow.

"Yes, Amy, I've been naughty!" exclaimed Lucy impetuously. She saw now how wrong she had been in allowing herself to be so led away by her ambition, as to have sacrificed to it all else, even her habit of watching in faith for

"The service that Thy love appoints."

Numerous instances rushed upon her mind, in which she had turned aside from opportunities of usefulness, of showing kindness and forbearance to others; she had been letting her oil run out and her lamp burnt faint and dim, and all that she might gain this petty prize, which she was likely to lose after all. Had she not, in yielding to her peculiar temptation, allowed herself to become as worldly as those whom in her heart she had been condemning?

Amy's gentle voice came to awaken more soothing thoughts. "But why do you cry so, Lucy?" she said. "Wont Jesus forgive you, and make you good?"

Lucy's "bread upon the waters" had come back to her in spiritual comfort, just when she most needed it. She put her arms round her little monitor, and as she kissed her, her thoughts formed an earnest prayer that her Lord would indeed forgive her, and help her to begin again, wiser for her experience, and strong in looking to him for strength.

The quiet hours which her headache enforced were of great service to her, in giving her time for thought and resolution. When at last she rose, and arranged her hair to go down stairs, her heart had grown so much lighter and calmer, that she felt more like herself than she had done for months, and she could now leave the matter of the prizes, without undue anxiety, with Him who knew what was best for her, and who, she was sure, would not refuse her any good thing.

The examination in history was the first to come off. When Lucy looked at the list of questions she found that several of them were on the part of the subject she had overlooked, and that these she could not answer at all. She felt that all chance of the prize was over, but she did not allow her mind to dwell on this circumstance, but wrote her replies to the other questions, with a calmness and clearness which would have been quite beyond her power, had she allowed herself to remain in a condition of feverish suspense.

When the examiners' decision was made known, it was found that the first prize had been awarded to Miss Eastwood, who was quite taken by surprise at receiving it; but that as Miss Raymond's paper had been so good in all except a very few points, the second prize, awarded to her, was considered almost equal to the first. This was much better than Lucy had expected, and as she received two first prizes in subjects where she had felt by no means sure of success, she was on the whole very well satisfied, as was Fred also, when her joyful letter informed him of the result.

Stella announced Lucy's success at home with almost as much pleasure as if the success had been her own. Edwin congratulated her with rather more animation than he was in the habit of showing, and Ada declared that "It must be nice to be so smart."

"Yes; but Lucy has been injuring her health by her close study," remarked the more observant Sophy. "Look at her now, how pale and thin she is, compared with what she was when she came."

"Oh, the holidays will set me all right again," Lucy declared, laughing; but Mrs. Brooke decided that Lucy needed immediate change of air. She had been hoping to be able to spend her holidays at Ashleigh, among her old friends; and as the Brookes were all going to a fashionable seaside resort, it seemed likely that nothing would occur to prevent the hoped-for visit. But Amy's cough, as well as other symptoms of delicacy of the lungs, had increased so much, that the doctor declared the sea-air too keen for her, and that she had better be sent, during the warm season, to a quiet, inland place in the neighborhood, the air of which he thought particularly suited to her constitution. But of course, Amy could not be sent there alone, and none of the rest would have been willing to give up their proposed visit to the seaside, except Mrs. Brooke, who could not be spared from her duties to her other daughters.

Lucy therefore seemed the one who should accompany Amy, and she herself felt that it was an occasion on which she might make some return for the kindness she had met with in her uncle's family. So her visit to Ashleigh was given up, and Amy's delight at finding that she was to accompany her to Oak Vale, was enough to make her forget any disappointment which her decision had involved. They were to be received into the family of a friend of the doctor's, a widow lady, who frequently received invalids as boarders, with whom little Amy would receive all the care and comfort she needed.

A few days before their departure, Lucy at last received, through Bessie Ford, the address of Nelly Connor's mistress. Stella, who, notwithstanding her raillery at Lucy's *protégée,* had a sort of latent interest in Nelly, from her association with her pleasant visit to Ashleigh, accompanied her cousin in her long walk, to look for the house. On reaching it at last, tired and hot, the door was opened, not by Nelly, as Lucy had hoped, but by an unprepossessing looking woman, whose hard face grew more rigid when informed what was the object of her visit.

"You needn't come here to look for her," she replied grimly; "she's left this sometime since, and I don't never want to set eyes on her again."

"Is she not here, then? Where is she gone?"

"I don't know," was the reply, "and I don't want to know. A girl that could behave as she done, to one who took such pains with her, and kept her so long, a'n't a girl to my taste. I wash my hands of her."

"But perhaps you could tell us what place she went to from you?" persisted Lucy. "I am a friend of hers, and would like to find her out."

"Well, she is no credit to her friends," said the woman, rather pleased at being able to give her a bad character where it might be of some consequence. "And as for the vagrant character she went off with, I'd be very sorry to have any acquaintance with him."

Finding the uselessness of prosecuting her inquiries there, Lucy bade Mrs. Williams good-day, feeling sure that Nelly's conduct had been misrepresented, an opinion shared by Stella, who had taken a strong dislike to the woman's grim demeanor and spiteful tone, and very sorry for having lost the only clue to her *protégée* once more.

XIII.

A FRIENDSHIP.

"We had been girlish friends
With hearts that, like the summer's half-oped buds
Grew close, and hived their sweetness for each other."

LUCY and Amy were soon settled in Mrs. Browne's pleasant little cottage at Oak Vale, a pretty sheltered village surrounded by hills clothed principally with noble oaks, whence it derived its name. Mrs. Browne's house lay a little way out of the village, amid green fields and lanes, which, after the hot, dusty city streets, were inexpressibly refreshing to Lucy, recalling old times at Ashleigh.

Mrs. Browne was a kind, motherly person, a doctor's widow, herself possessing a good deal of medical skill, which rendered her house especially eligible for invalids, and she established a careful watch over little Amy, whose very precarious condition her practised eye saw at a glance. Whenever, the child, feeling better than usual, would have overtasked her failing strength in the quiet country rambles which were such a delightful novelty to one who had scarcely ever been really in the country before, and when Lucy's inexperience might have allowed her to injure herself without knowing it, Mrs. Browne would interpose a gentle warning, which was always cheerfully obeyed. It was with some surprise, indeed, that she noticed with what perfect submission the little girl bore all the deprivations of innocent pleasure which her weak state compelled, as well as the feverish languor which often oppressed her in the hot August days. This submission arose from the implicit belief which, child as she was, she had, that everything that befell her was ordered by the kind Saviour, who would send nothing that was not for her real good. Such a belief, fully realized, would soon relieve most of us from the fretting cares and corroding anxieties that arise from our "taking thought" about things we cannot control.

"I never saw a child like her," Mrs. Browne would say; "indeed, she's more like an angel than a child, and it's my belief she'll soon be one in reality. And I'm sure heaven's more the place for her than this rough world."

However, Amy seemed to improve under the healthful influences of Oak Vale, living almost wholly in the fresh open air, perfumed with mignonette and other sweet summer flowers, sitting with Lucy, under the trees before Mrs. Browne's house, or in her shady verandah, where, even on the warmest day, there was a breeze to cool the sultry air. Lucy would read to her, sometimes some of Longfellow's simpler poems, out of one of her prize-books, and sometimes out of more juvenile story-books brought down for Amy's benefit, who was never tired of hearing her favorites read over and over again, to which she would listen with an abstracted, thoughtful expression, as if she were interpreting the story in a spiritual fashion of her own. "Heaven is about us in our infancy," says the poet, and it is nearer to some children, by the grace of God, than older people often imagine.

When Lucy wanted to read to herself, Amy would amuse herself quietly for hours, dressing her dolls, and looking over the illustrations in her story-books, supplying the story from memory. Lucy conscientiously kept up her practising on Mrs. Browne's piano, and always ended by playing and singing some hymns for Amy, who was passionately fond of music, and loved to try to sing, too, with her sweet feeble voice.

As Mrs. Browne, having but one servant, had a great deal to do herself, Lucy volunteered to assist her a little. She had always been accustomed to perform some household tasks at home, and it was quite an amusement to her and Amy, bringing back old days of her childhood, to vary their mornings by shelling the peas for dinner, or, when it was not too warm, picking the fruit for Mrs. Browne's preserves. So pleasant did Lucy find it, that she thought her city cousins really missed a good deal of enjoyment, in never, by any chance, employing themselves in anything of the kind, even when the busy servants were really overworked. Indeed, it is somewhat surprising, that domestics go on as contentedly as they do in their constant treadmill of labor, often too much for their strength, when so many healthy members of the families for whose benefit they toil, spend so large a portion of their time in luxurious idleness, or in mere pleasure-seeking.

In the fresh cool morning, after their early breakfast, and in the evening, when the heat of the day was over, Lucy and Amy always went for a short ramble, climbing a little way up one of the hill-paths, or wandering by the side of the stream, which, fringed with elm and birch, wound through the village that lay on both sides of it, the river being crossed in two or three places by rustic bridges. From the point on the hillside which generally formed the limit of their walk, and where they used to sit on a mossy stone to rest, they had an extensive view over the surrounding country, diversified with cornfields, orchards, and deep green woods, and dotted with farm-houses, while close at their feet lay the white cluster of village-houses, with a few of higher pretensions scattered here and there on the green slopes by the river-side, among their shrubberies and embowering trees.

The fields were beginning to wear the deeper and richer hues of approaching autumn, and it was a perpetual pleasure to watch the rippling motion of the golden grain waving in the breeze, or the rapid changes of light and shade on the fields and woods, as the clouds passed swiftly over the sky. To watch these were their morning pleasures; but better still, perhaps, they loved the quiet sunset hours, when the glowing tints of the sky seemed to clothe the landscape in an unearthly glory, and then, gradually, each bright hue would fade out from the sky and from the land below, leaving the scene to the solemn repose of the shadowy evening, broken only by the flitting fireflies, or to the flood of silver light shed by the rising moon. But Amy was never to be allowed to be out in the night air, so that their rambles had to be over before the damp night dews. They generally found Mrs.

Browne standing at the gate, awaiting their return, anxious lest her charge should have ventured to remain out too long.

More than a week of their stay had passed rapidly by, when, one evening that Lucy and Amy were spending in wandering by the river, the former suddenly recognized approaching them, the familiar form of her classmate, Miss Eastwood, the winner of the first History prize. The recognition was, of course, mutual, and in the surprise of meeting so unexpectedly, and in explanations of how it had come about, the two girls exchanged more words than they had ever done when in the same classes at Mrs. Wilmot's.

"And you did not know Oakvale was my home," said Mary Eastwood, when Lucy had told how she and her cousin came to be there. Lucy had never heard where Miss Eastwood's home was, and it had not occurred to her to connect the Dr. Eastwood, of whom Mrs. Browne often spoke, with the name of her classmate. Mary showed them her father's house, beautifully situated on the opposite sloping bank of the river, which, with its shady trees and white gate, reminded her a good deal of her own old home, though the house was larger and handsomer. Dr. Eastwood, who was with his daughter, looked at little Amy with a good deal of interest, asking a number of questions, while he held her delicate hand in his, and watched her fair pale face with his keen eye. He and Mary walked back with them to Mrs. Browne's cottage, promising to come and see them soon, and inviting them to visit Mary.

This unexpected rencontre greatly added to Lucy's enjoyment of her stay at Oakvale. The cousins very soon had the pleasure of spending an afternoon in Dr. Eastwood's family, a Christian household, after Lucy's own heart. Now that the first stiffness of their school-relations had been brushed off by the surprise of their meeting, the two girls found each other delightful companions, and soon became fast friends. It was the first time Lucy had ever found a congenial companion of her own sex, and their friendship afforded a new and ever-increasing delight. They saw each other every day, and often spent the long summer mornings, alike pleasantly and profitably, in reading aloud by turns, from some interesting and improving book out of Dr. Eastwood's excellent library. Mrs. Eastwood often sat by, also enjoying the reading, and by her judicious remarks, directing the minds of her young companions to profitable thought. The book selected was often a religious one, such as some people would have considered only fit for Sundays; but it was not the less interesting to them on that account, and gave rise to some of their happiest discussions, when each perceived, with delight, how thoroughly the other could appreciate and reciprocate her own deepest feelings. Little Amy would listen attentively at such times, showing, by her interest, that she comprehended more of what was said than could have been expected. But whenever Mrs. Eastwood thought the conversation beyond her depth, or her mind too much excited, she would send her away to play with her own younger children, who were always glad to place all their toys at her disposal, and do all in their power for her amusement.

At Dr. Eastwood's the readings generally went on under a spreading walnut-tree on the lawn, and Amy would roam at large with the children, or come and rest within hearing, just as she liked. Sometimes she would lie still for hours on the cushions which Mrs. Eastwood had laid on the grass for her benefit, gazing through the flickering green leaves into the blue depths of the sky, her earnest eyes looking as if they penetrated beyond things visible, and held communion with thoughts not suggested by any mortal voice.

Often in the afternoons, while Amy was safe and happy with her little friends, Mary and Lucy would take a walk of some miles, carrying perhaps some message or comfort for some of Dr. Eastwood's poor patients, or driving with him on some of his distant rounds, or rowing in a boat on the river with one of Mary's brothers, to gather water-lilies, and bring home their snowy or golden flowers in their waxlike beauty, to delight little Amy, who was sensitively alive to all natural loveliness.

During these expeditions the two girls discussed almost every conceivable topic of mutual interest, and gave each other the history of their previous lives, though Mary's had flowed on almost as uneventfully as Lucy's had done, previous to her father's death. They compared notes as to their favorite books, poetry, and theories, their tastes being sufficiently different to give rise to many a pleasant, good-humored controversy. Sometimes, when deeper chords were touched, they confided to each other some of their spiritual history; what influences had first brought them to know a Saviour's love, and then led their hearts to him who had given himself for them. Mary, who had a little class of her own at Oakvale, listened with much interest to the account of Miss Preston's parting words to her class, and the influence they had had on her scholars.

About her dear departed father, too, and the beloved home-circle, Lucy had much to tell. She said much less about the Brooke family; and Mary, who could understand how little congenial was the atmosphere of her uncle's house, respected her reticence. Lucy felt that she had no right to communicate any unfavorable impression of those from whom she had received so much kindness, and whose hospitality and kindness she had enjoyed so long.

"I always felt as if I wanted to know you better, Mary, when we were at Mrs. Wilmot's," said Lucy one evening, as they were returning home from a woodland walk, laden with wild-flowers and ferns. Mary colored a little, and hesitated.

"I'm afraid I was very stiff and selfish, Lucy dear," she replied, "but mamma used to give me so many cautions about mingling with worldly people, that I thought it was best to keep apart from them altogether; and I was told Mr. Brooke's family were so gay and worldly that I supposed you must be so too; and so I thought I ought not to get into any intimacy that might lead me into temptation."

"I suppose it is right to try to keep out of temptation," said Lucy thoughtfully.

"Yes, but now I can see that I was n't right in being so distrustful as to be afraid of what came naturally in my way. Mamma says that to be afraid of what may involve temptation, when God's providence, rightfully construed, leads us into it, is something like the dread which keeps people from doing their duty in cases of infection; whereas they should trust that, so long as they do not expose themseves to it wilfully and needlessly, God will care for them in the path by which he leads them, as well as in circumstances which look more secure."

"Yes, I'm sure that's true," said Lucy, thinking of what Fred had said to her when she had felt afraid to venture into the temptations of her uncle's house. "But then, whenever we get over our fear and feel secure, we are sure to fall into some snare."

"Yes," replied her friend, "because we forget our own dependence on Christ for strength, and begin to walk in our own, instead of looking to him continually for help."

"Do you know," said Lucy, "one of my greatest temptations was studying for the History prize! I was so determined to have it—so set upon it—that I let it come before everything else, and forgot to ask to be kept from temptation in it, till, just before the examination, I found I had forgotten part of what was to be studied; and then, in my disappointment, I found out how wrong I had been."

"Oh," exclaimed Mary, "I was almost sorry I got the first prize—which I hadn't been expecting at all—for I was sure you would be dreadfully disappointed. You had worked so hard for it; harder than I did."

"No, I wasn't disappointed then; I was sure I shouldn't get it, and didn't expect even the second prize; and I felt quite satisfied that it should be so, for I had been working in so wrong a spirit, that I could not have felt happy in getting the prize that had led me astray."

"Well, it's a relief to my mind to hear you say so," replied Mary, laughing, "for I felt quite guilty whenever I looked at that book, feeling as if I had by some incomprehensible accident taken it from the one who really deserved it."

Mary had as yet known but few temptations. Her life had been so calm and sheltered that she had had no experience of contrary winds, and her natural disposition was so equable that she had very little consciously to struggle against. Perhaps her chief temptation lay in a tendency to placid contemplative Christianity, without sufficient active interest in others; and Lucy's opposite qualities acted as a counteracting stimulus, while Mary's peaceful spirit of trusting faith calmed and soothed Lucy's rather impatient disposition. Thus in all true, loving, Christian companionship we may help each other on, making up what is lacking in one another by mutual edification.

One warm Sunday evening, after a very sultry day, Lucy and Amy were sitting together in Mrs. Browne's verandah. Mary had just left them, having walked home with Lucy from the evening service, and they had been discussing the sermon, which had been chiefly on sin and its hatefulness in the sight of God, as well as upon the fountain opened to remove it. After she was gone they had sat for some time in silence, watching the fire-flies glancing in and out of the dark trees. Suddenly Amy said, "Lucy, do you expect to go to heaven when you die, for sure?"

"I am quite sure there is nothing to prevent my going there," said Lucy, "for I know Jesus is able and willing to take me there."

"Shall I go there when I die, Lucy?" she asked, with a solemn earnestness that went to her cousin's heart.

"Why should you not, dear Amy, when Jesus died that you might?"

"But 'God will not look upon sin,' the Bible says, and I have a sinful heart; I feel it," replied the child.

"Well, why should Jesus have died for you if you had not? It was just to take away sin that Jesus came to suffer!'

"But it isn't taken away; I know it's there!" persisted Amy, who had evidently been distressing herself with the question how a heart, sinful on earth, could be fit for the pure atmosphere of heaven.

Lucy explained, to the best of her knowledge and ability, that while sin still clings to our mortal natures, Jesus has broken its power for ever, and taken away its condemnation, so that when we receive him into our hearts by faith, God no longer looks upon us as sinful and rebellious children, but as reconciled through the blood of Christ. And the same blood will also purify our hearts; and when soul and body are for ever separated, the last stain of sin will be taken away from the ransomed spirit.

Amy listened, and seemed satisfied; at least she never recurred to the subject, and, so far as Lucy knew, it was the last time that any perplexing doubts clouded the sunshine of her happy childlike faith.

Pleasant as were the days of their stay at Oakvale, they came at last, like all earthly things, to an end. The warm August weather had passed away, and the September breezes blew cool and fresh, permitting them to ramble about with comfort, even during the hours which they had before been obliged to spend entirely in the shade. The seaside party had already been settled at home for a week or two; before it was thought advisable that Amy should be brought back to the city. At last, however, the summons came, and Lucy spent the last two or three days in re-visiting for the last time all the favorite haunts where she had spent so many happy hours. She and her friend did not, however, permit themselves to repine at the ending of what had been to them both such a very delightful resting-place in their life-journey; since

> "Not enjoyment and not sorrow
> Is our destined end or way;
> But to live, that each to-morrow
> Finds us farther than to-day."

Mary, who had delayed her own return to school, on her friend's account, was to accompany them to town, to begin her last year at Mrs. Wilmot's.

Amy had seemed so well during their stay at Oakvale that Lucy had become hopeful of her complete recovery. But Dr. Eastwood warned her that the improvement might be merely temporary, and that in any case it was, in his judgment, impossible that Amy could ever be quite strong and well. "And I don't know," he said kindly to Lucy, who felt a sharp pang at the thought of losing her dear little cousin, "that it is well to set your heart on the prolongation of a life which can scarcely be anything but one of weakness and suffering."

So with many mingled feelings of hope and fear and regret, and many kind farewells from all their Oakvale friends, the young party took their departure, and found themselves soon again among city sights and sounds.

XIV.

AN UNEXPECTED RECOGNITION.

"For love's a flower that will not die
 For lack of leafy screen;
And Christian hope can cheer the eye
 That ne'er saw vernal green.
Then, be ye sure that Love can bless
Even in this crowded loneliness,
Where ever-moving myriads seem to say,
Go! thou art naught to us, nor we to thee; away!"

MR. BROOKE met the young travellers at the station, anxious about his youngest daughter, whose improved appearance he was much pleased to note; and Stella met them at the door with every demonstration of delight. "It has been so dull here without you," she exclaimed; "the house seems so quiet, after all the fun we have been having at the seaside. I've been teasing papa to let me go for you, and I would have gone if you hadn't come soon!"

She was looking prettier than ever, Lucy thought: so blooming and gay and graceful after her seaside sojourn. Her cousin could not wonder that she won her way to most people's hearts, and was forced to admit the contrast between her and her fragile little sister, whose faint bloom even now did not remove the appearance of ill-health. But there was on her pale face a spiritual beauty—a repose and peace which Stella, in all the loveliness of a pure rose-tinted complexion, lustrous eyes, and gleaming golden hair, did not possess. It was the reflection, outwardly, of the "peace of God which passeth understanding."

Stella talked all the evening without ceasing, and at night accompanied Lucy to her room, there to go on talking still, enlarging, in a lively, amusing strain, on the adventures of their seaside life, the "fun," the "splendid bathing," the people who were there, their

AN UNEXPECTED RECOGNITION. 247

dress, manners, and conversation; all the flirtations she had observed, with the quick eye of a girl who as yet has no personal interest in such matters. When, at last, Stella paused in her own narration to ask questions about Oakvale, Lucy gladly took advantage of the break to insist on postponing all further conversation until the morrow, especially as, she urged, they were keeping Amy from the sleep she needed so much after her long journey, and accustomed as she had lately been to early hours. Lucy, indeed, felt determined that the same thing must not happen again, on any account, as the consequences to Amy -of having her mind and nervous system excited so late at night, when she was always too much disposed to wakefulness, might be exceedingly injurious.

"Oh, how I wish Stella were more like dear Mary," thought Lucy, as she laid her head on her pillow and compared Mary's kind thoughtfulness with Stella's impulsive, flighty giddiness. As to externals, Stella had very much the advantage, for Mary Eastwood could not be called pretty, and was rather reserved in manner with those whom she did not know well; but Lucy could not help feeling Mary's great superiority as a companion, when she compared the state of mind in which Stella's stream of gossip had left her, with the elevating, stimulating tendency of her conversations with Mary on subjects more worthy of immortal beings. They seemed mutually to draw each other on to a sphere far above the petty frivolities on which so many fritter away powers given for higher ends. Even when they did not touch on topics directly religious, they seemed to be far nearer the Light that is "inaccessible and full of glory," when discussing the working of God's laws and providence in nature and history, than if their minds had been lowered and discolored by dwelling on the faults, follies, and petty concerns of their neighbors.

Sophy, who had been a little fagged and worn out by her incessant round of gayety, previous to her going to the seaside, was now looking more brilliantly handsome, Lucy thought, than she had ever seen her. Stella had informed her that Sophy's betrothed had been at the seaside with them. "And oh! he's so delightful! You can't think! so handsome and good-natured and obliging! I can tell you, Sophy looked proud of him there! He gave her the loveliest emerald set; you'll see her wear them; and I'm pretty sure they're to be married next spring, though she wont tell me; but I'll coax it out of Ada."

Lucy thought Sophy must be very happy, yet she could not help thinking, if both she and her lover were really Christians, how much happier they would be. Nothing Stella had said led her to suppose that he was; and if he were, what an alloy of anxiety and separation in the most important points would mar the perfection of love!

It was with increased zest, and a fuller appreciation of the interest and value of her studies, that Lucy entered upon them once more. The happy weeks at Oakvale had been of permanent benefit to her in opening new channels of thought and enlarging her sphere of mental vision, both through the books she had been reading and the comments of Dr. and Mrs. Eastwood, both of whom had thoughtful, cultivated minds. She now studied with very little reference to prizes, or even the approbation of masters, but from a deep interest in the studies themselves, and a feeling of their beneficial effect in leading her to higher ranges of thought. Every new attainment was but a step to a fresh starting-point in the never-ending pursuit of knowledge; and Longfellow's beautiful lines often recurred to her mind—

> "The lofty pyramids of stone
> That, wedge-like, cleave the desert airs,
> When nearer seen and better known,
> Are but gigantic flights of stairs."

Then the feeling grew to be more and more strong with her; that every new acquisition—every step in mental discipline which God had given her the opportunity of making—was a talent to be held in trust and used in his service. Mrs. Eastwood had explained that, though we may often have to study during the years of school-life without seeing what special use we may be called to make of our acquisitions, still God will undoubtedly find some use for whatever power we have gained while following the leading of his providence. "Therefore," she would say, "the doubt whether such and such a thing will ever be of any use to us is no excuse for sloth in acquiring it, when it is clearly our duty to do so."

Her studies were rendered doubly interesting by the companionship of Mary Eastwood, who was animated by the same spirit, and in whose friendship she found her greatest pleasure during the winter. Stella was rather surprised at the affectionate greeting between her cousin and Miss Eastwood the first day they met at school, for she had scarcely given Lucy an opportunity of telling her more than than that they had met often at Oakvale.

"Well! to think of your having all at once struck up such a violent friendship with that stiff, quiet Miss Eastwood!" exclaimed Stella, who thought her cousin's choice of a friend rather unaccountable. Lucy's efforts to draw together her cousin and her friend were unsuccessful, and perhaps this was quite as much Mary's fault as Stella's, arising from her strong feeling against cultivating intimacy with any one who was "of the world." It was almost the only practical point on which she and Lucy disagreed, for Lucy tried to persuade her that she might do real good, if she would come more in contact with her irreligious schoolmates. But Mary replied that this might do for some, but she did not feel strong enough; she might herself be led away. She was not yet fully persuaded in her own mind.

So Lucy gave up the point, and had a somewhat difficult position to maintain between her cousin and her friend; not that Mary was ever jealous, but Stella did not at all like the affection of her friends to be diverted towards any one else; indeed, it was the only thing that ever seemed really to "put her out." She was conscious to some extent that a much deeper sympathy existed between Lucy and Miss Eastwood than between Lucy and her, and she feared that if it increased, her cousin's regard for her must necessarily diminish.

One bright, sunny October day, when the air was clear and bracing, and the wind was tossing the red leaves that fell from the trees in the squares, Lucy and Stella were on their

AN UNEXPECTED RECOGNITION. 253

way home from school, when they heard at a slight distance the plaintive strains of a hand-organ, carried by a meagre, care-worn Italian, who seemed to be working his instrument mechanically, while his eye had a fixed, sad, steadfast gaze, unconscious, seemingly, of anything around him. Lucy was looking compassionately at the dark, sorrowful face, and wondering what his previous history might have been, when her eye was suddenly caught by the familiar form and face of the girl who stood by with her tambourine, singing a simple ditty, which somehow brought old days at Ashleigh back to her mind. The figure she saw, though arrayed in tattered garments, and the face, though sunburnt to a deep brown, were not so much altered as to prevent almost instant recognition. Lucy grasped Stella's arm, and exclaimed, "Why, it's Nelly!" and before the astonished Stella comprehended her meaning, she hastily stepped forward towards the tambourine-girl, who almost at the same moment stopped singing and sprang forward, exclaiming, "Oh, it's Miss Lucy, her own self!"

Both were quite unconscious, in their surprise, of the bystanders around them; but Stella was by no means so insensible to the situation, and was somewhat scandalized at being connected with such a scene "in the street." She begged Lucy to ask Nelly to follow them home, which was not far off, and then they could have any number of explanations at leisure. Lucy at once assented, and asked Nelly if she could be spared for a little while. With a happy face, flushed with her surprise and delight, Nelly went up to the organ-grinder and said a few words, at which he smiled and nodded. She then followed her friends home at a respectful distance, while the man went on his way from house to house.

Nelly's explanation of her present odd circumstances was very simple, and, on the whole, satisfactory. In the hot July weather, when she felt her over-tasked strength failing, and could scarcely manage to drag herself about to perform her daily round of duty, often scolded for doing it inefficiently, the poor organ-grinder came one day with a face more sorrowful than ever, and told Nelly, weeping, that his daughter—his *povera picciola*—had been carried off by one of those sudden attacks that so soon run their course and snap the thread of weakly lives. He was so lonely now, he said, he could not bear it! Would Nelly come and be his daughter and take poor Teresa's forsaken tambourine? She had a voice sweet as Teresa's own, and he would teach her to sing when he played. She should have no hard work, and no scolding, and they would take care of each other.

It was a tempting offer to poor Nelly, pining under continual chilling indifference and fault-finding. While she was hesitating, her mistress, hearing a strange voice in the kitchen, came down in wrath to dismiss the intruder, who rose instantly at the sound of her harsh voice. "I go, signora," he said, in his foreign English, "and this girl goes with me. You give her too hard work, and hard words. I will take care for her, and she shall be to me as the *povera* who is dead! Come, *picciola!*"

Mrs. Williams had by this time so far recovered from her amazement as to find voice enough to demand of Nelly whether she was really going to be so ungrateful as to leave a place where she had been so kindly treated, and ruin herself for life, by going off with a wandering character like that. But Nelly's reply was ready. "You said, ma'am, you'd have to send me away because I couldn't do your work properly. So I think I'd better go."

And hurriedly collecting her few possessions she was ready in two minutes to accompany her newly-found protector. Mrs. Williams endeavored to detain her, threatening to "take the law of her." But Nelly was determined. Anything was better than remaining there, and Mrs. Williams, who was somewhat overawed by the Italian's determined eye, gave up what she saw was a vain attempt. She shut the door after them with expressive force, and then went up stairs to discourse to her daughter on the incredible ingratitude and heartlessness of such creatures.

Nelly had faithfully served Mrs. Williams to the utmost of her strength and ability for

AN UNEXPECTED RECOGNITION. 257

five months, and her mistress had in return given her food of the poorest quality, and one old print dress of her own, worn almost to tatters. Yet Mrs. Williams, having herself a pretty hard struggle to make both ends meet, was at least more excusable than those who, themselves abounding in wealth and luxury, grind down, so far as they can, the poor hirelings who may be in their power.

Since then Nelly had faithfully followed the poor Italian whom at his own desire she called "*padre.*" It did not to her mean the same as "father," nor would she have given to any one else the name sacred to her own unforgotten father. But she was to the poor man as a daughter, and her brown face, though still thin had lost the pining, wistful look which had been previously habitual to it. Lucy observed the glow of pleasure that lighted up her face when she heard again the familiar sound of the organ in the distance. The *padre* was very good to her, she said, and though they often had long weary rounds with a scant allowance of pennies, they always had enough to eat; and hitherto it had been very pleasant, and she had no hard scrubbing or washing to do.

"I'd have died soon, Miss Lucy, if I'd stayed at Mrs. Williams'. Was it wrong to come away?"

Lucy could not say it was, in spite of the irregularity of the precedent.

"But the *padre* wont be able to go about in the winter time, Miss Lucy, for he has such a cough, and pain in his breast, whenever he gets wet or cold, and some days he's hardly able to play his organ, and then I don't know what he'll do. What could I do, Miss Lucy, to help him?"

Lucy promised to consider the matter. She had obtained leave to give the organ-grinder and Nelly a good substantial meal in the kitchen, which was greatly relished by both. She took down the name of the street in which they lived, and got a minute description of the house, promising soon to visit them. The man was, evidently, far from strong, and his bright, hollow eye, and haggard face, sometimes unnaturally flushed, betokened too surely incipient disease.

AN UNEXPECTED RECOGNITION. 259

"And why did you never come to see me, Nelly? You knew where I was," said Lucy, as they were going away.

"O Miss Lucy," exclaimed Nelly eagerly, "but I did, three times, but you were n't in; I was ashamed to come any more. The last times, they said you were away in the country."

"But why did n't you leave word where you were living, and I would have found you out?"

"O Miss Lucy, I could n't think you 'd be at the trouble of coming to see me!"

"Well, I will come, though, now I know where you live," said Lucy, as she bade them good-by.

Little Amy had been very much interested in the history of Nelly, as Lucy had told it to her, and had come down to see her. She stood by, putting her thin hand on hers, and looking up wonderingly in her face, exciting Nelly's compassion and interest by her sweet, delicate look. "She's more like an angel than Miss Stella, though I used to think her like one," thought Nelly.

Amy asked many questions about Nelly and the "poor man," and begged Lucy to take her when she went to see them. But so long a walk was out of the question for Amy, nor would her mother have consented to let either her or Stella go to such a quarter of the city. Even Lucy's going was a matter for some consideration, but she begged hard to be allowed to fulfil her promise. At last Edwin good-naturedly said he "didn't mind going with Lucy, to see that she wasn't carried off for her clothes, like the little girl in the story-books; and they made the expedition together, her cousin waiting outside, while Lucy paid her most welcome visit.

They found the place a very quiet one, and the street, though poor, not at all disreputable. Edwin gave the best account of it he could, that Lucy might be able in future, without his escort, to visit Nelly, as she occasionally did, accompanied by her friend Mary Eastwood, who sometimes spent the Saturday afternoon with her at Mr. Brooke's. Their visits and little gifts of money were very timely, for the poor organ-grinder was grow-

AN UNEXPECTED RECOGNITION. 261

ing less and less able to persevere in his uncertain calling; and though Nelly was practising plainsewing, that she might be able to earn something herself, it was not likely that her exertions could bring in much.

In these visits to Nelly, the two friends soon found out other poor people in the same locality, even more urgently needing a kind word, and a helping hand. In work of this kind, as in most other things, "it is only the first step which costs." One has only to make a beginning, and straightway one case leads to another, and that interest grows with the work, until, to some happy and highly-privileged people, it really becomes their meat and drink, thus to do their Father's business.

This new kind of work was a great interest to Lucy, and in planning how best to aid the poor in whom she was interested, and in diligent and happy study, the autumn months passed rapidly away.

XV.

THE FLOWER FADETH.

"And yet, his words mean more than they,
And yet, he owns their praise;
Why should we think He turns away
From infants' simple lays?"

AS the autumn deepened into winter, bringing cold, damp days, and chilling, keen winds, little Amy's strength seemed steadily to decrease, notwithstanding all the care taken to reinforce it by the most nourishing diet that money could command. Every delicacy that could tempt her appetite, every kind of nourishment that could strengthen her system, was tried, without success. Dr. Eastwood had been right in his augury, that her seeming improvement had been only temporary, and that the delicately organized constitution was not meant for the wear and tear of long life. So evident, at last, did the decline become, that a consultation was held as to whether it would not be advisable to remove her for the winter to a warmer climate; but the more experienced physicians were decidedly of opinion that taking her away from her home and family would be a needless cruelty, and that since no human skill could now arrest the disease, it was better to leave the little patient to live, as long as she might, surrounded by the comforts and the kind nursing at home. This opinion was not fully communicated to her parents, but they instinctively felt, what was really the case, that their child was only left in their home because she must ere long be removed from it for ever.

Lucy had long taught herself to think of such an issue as at least a probability; but her cousins by no means realized the advanced state of Amy's disease. They persuaded themselves that, with care, she would "get over" her delicacy, and they would not even think of the possibility of a fatal termination of it. One cause of this was, probably, the circumstance that the winter gayeties had commenced, and that invitations, parties, and dress, were now uppermost in their minds. Had they been convinced that their little sister was dying, they could hardly have had the heart to join in their usual round of gayety; but they easily persuaded themselves of the contrary, and felt no scruples about going on as usual.

Stella, who had shot up almost to womanly height within the last year, had assumed the dress and appearance of a "young lady," as distinguished from a little girl. The foretaste of gay life she had had at the seaside, had made her impatient to plunge into it at once, and she besieged her parents with entreaties that she might be allowed to "come out" that winter. She succeeded so far with her father, who could seldom deny her anything, as to obtain leave to go to as many private parties as she could, without interfering with her studies. But, of course, with a limit so indefinite, the bounds were often overstepped. Her love of gayety only grew with the indulgence of the taste, and she felt really unhappy

THE FLOWER FADETH. 265

when she had to see her sisters go to a party without her.

But late hours and excitement very soon affected a constitution which had never before been so severely tried; and as she would conceal any indisposition when she thought it might keep her at home, the consequences sometimes became serious. At last her rashness in going out, thinly dressed one cold winter evening, when she was already suffering from a slight cold, brought on a severe attack of inflammation of the lungs, by which she was prostrated for several weeks, and which left behind a slight cough. This, the doctor warned her, would require the utmost care, to prevent its growing into what might prove very serious indeed.

Lucy, of course, owing to her deep mourning, and the school-work which engrossed her mind and time, had had no temptation to mingle in any of her cousins' amusements, though, had it been otherwise, she could not conscientiously have frequented scenes of amusement which she had been taught by her father to consider unworthy of those who have made up their minds to leave all and follow Christ. For the same reason, she had refused Stella's urgent solicitations to accompany her in occasional visits to the opera and theatre, places of which her father had often told her the spiritual atmosphere was entirely foreign to that in which Christians should seek ever to dwell. Though Stella's glowing descriptions sometimes excited the longing to see the magic sights and hear the magnificent music of which they told, she felt that she could not sincerely pray, "lead us not into temptation," if she wilfully went into it; nor could she from the heart have asked her Saviour's blessing on the evening's amusement?

During the general engrossment of the household with Stella's alarming attack, Amy's rapid sinking of strength was not for some time much noticed, except by Lucy, who felt, in spite of her hopes, that the end was drawing near.

Lucy had been forbidden to speak to her little cousin about death, as if the avoidance of the thought could have anything to do with delaying the event; but happily there was no need for doing so, since her little heart was evidently resting on her Saviour, and she was thus prepared for whatever he should send her. Her childlike faith, and her vivid realization of heavenly things, seemed to grow stronger as her bodily strength failed, and though she never specially referred to death, the approach of which a child is not able to realize, her mind was evidently full of thoughts about heaven, about its glories and occupations, about Him who is "the Resurrection and the Life." She was always asking questions about the childhood of Jesus; questions which Lucy often found it impossible to answer, and was never tired of hearing the few passages in the New Testament which referred to it.

Some instances of childish sin seemed to weigh upon her conscience; but Lucy reminded her that the Lamb of God had washed away her sins with his own blood, and that the moment we come to him by faith, we are sure of the forgiveness of past sin, as well as of deliverance from its present power. This perfectly satisfied her, and nothing else seemed to trouble her.

The little girl was intensely interested in the poor Italian, who was sinking almost as fast as she was. He seldom now stirred from his chair in the warmest corner of the room, and his cough had become terribly harassing, especially at night. His breathing, too, was much oppressed, and poor Nelly had often a heavy heart, as the conviction forced itself upon her that she was about to lose the kind friend and protector, around whom her warm heart had closely entwined itself. She tried hard to earn a little for his support and her own, by the sewing which she occasionally got, often from people nearly as poor as herself; but her utmost exertions in this way would not have sufficed to keep them from starvation, had it not been for the timely aid brought by Lucy, and by Mary Eastwood, whose well-supplied purse was always ready to furnish what was needed for their comfort. Lucy had very little to give of her own, but Mrs. Brooke was sufficiently interested in her account of the case to be very willing to help, for she was not at all indisposed to benevolent actions, if she had had the energy to discover the way. Amy, too, always insisted that a portion of the delicacies prepared for her should be kept for "the poor organ-grinder," and one of her greatest pleasures was in hearing from Lucy how the invalid liked what had been sent him, and how gratefully he sent his thanks to the little "signorina." She asked Lucy whether the poor man loved Jesus, and would go to heaven when he died, and seemed much grieved at hearing of his praying to the Virgin, the mother of Jesus.

"What a pity," she would say, "for she can't hear him, nor save him, can she? And so his prayers will be of no use."

She lay still for a short time, considering the matter, and then said, as if a ray of comfort had come to her. "But Jesus can hear him, and perhaps He will give him what he needs, though he didn't ask Him."

Lucy would hope so, too, and agree with her, that when he got to heaven he would know better. For she had reason to believe, notwithstanding Antonio's prayers to the Virgin, the remnant of the superstitious faith he had held from childhood, that he was nevertheless gradually coming to the knowledge of the Saviour as the only mediator and sacrifice for sin. Nelly's treasured card was fastened up conspicuously in their little room, and the rich colors in which the text, "Looking unto Jesus," was printed, pleased the Italian's southern love of color, and led his eye often to rest upon it, as he spent the long hours sitting wearily in his chair. And gradually he came to attach some real meaning to the words which at first he had regarded merely as a pleasant thing to look at. Nelly would sometimes tell him some of the things Miss Preston said to her about it, which clung tenaciously to her memory, and how the thought that Jesus was her Friend and Saviour, to whom she must always look in her need, had been her one comfort when left friendless and alone. She often read to him a chapter out of the little Bible which was Lucy's parting gift when she left Ashleigh, and had, ever since, been Nelly's dearest treasure. And he would always listen with deep interest to the history of the wonderful life which has come home to the hearts of thousands in all the centuries which have elapsed since it was lived among the hills and valleys of Palestine. He loved to hear Nelly sing, in her rich, sweet voice, her favorite hymn, "I lay my sins on Jesus," and would sometimes try to join in the strains himself, as well as his feebleness would let him. He showed his appreciation of the motto, in his own way, by placing his crucifix above the card, and he would sit for hours gazing silently at both.

Lucy, in her frequent visits, often read to him the passages which bear most directly on the love of Christ, and the full and free forgiveness of sin through him; and she sometimes added simple comments of her own, preferring, however, in general, to leave God's words to work their own way into his heart. His church prejudices she never ventured to touch feeling that to do so might arouse them, against the reception of the simple gospel, and do him harm by exciting his mind injuriously and bewildering him with conflicting opinions. She avoided all collision with ideas which had been so long closely intertwined with the only ideas of religion he had, feeling sure that the light of gospel truth, once introduced into the heart, would sooner or later disperse the darkness of error by its own power.

Except for the one dark foreboding that became, month by month, and week by week, more distinct, these would have been very happy days for Nelly. Her warm Irish heart found scope for its action, in continually ministering to the comfort of one to whom she was bound by ties of love and gratitude, and no harsh or unkind word now fell upon her ear. The poor Italian, always of a gentle nature, except when influenced by passion, had ever treated her with indulgent kindness, and she had given him her warm affection in return. Her assiduous attentions were labors of love, and so was the needlework at which she stitched away with diligent though unpractised hands. Coarse, hard sewing it was; but Nelly did not mind that, in the feeling that she was earning something, however small. While she sat plying her needle, through the short days and long evenings of the winter, the invalid's thoughts would wander back to long past, but unforgotten days, and he would amuse Nelly with little bits of his past history. He would describe, over and over again, his childhood's home in·the lovely *Riviera*, where the intense azure of the sky, and the pure sapphire of the Mediterranean, contrasted sharply with the white glitter of the rocks as they emerged in bold relief from their drapery of rich, deep-hued vegetation. He would tell her about the white Italian village nestling among the vine-clad terraces and sloping hillsides clad with olive and myrtle, and about the trellised house where he was born, and his father's little vineyard where the rich purple and amber clusters, such as little Amy now sent him as costly luxuries, hung down in rich masses which any hand could pick. Such descriptions were intensely fascinating to Nelly's quick Celtic imagination, and she would speak in her turn of the breezy slopes by the sea where she had so often played in days she could still vividly remember; of the aromatic scent of the burning heaps of sea-weed, whose smouldering fires she used to fan; of the fresh bracing sea-air, and dancing blue waves with their snowy crests of foam, and the distant white sails winging their way to some unknown haven.

Their talk always took a sadder tone when the Italian spoke of his later life, and told how he left his quiet village, hoping to make his fortune in the great world as a musician; how his hopes had been gradually crushed down, and he wandered from place to place till he emigrated to America, where the deadly cholera carried off his wife and her infant boy, leaving him only his little daughter; how, since then, dispirited and weary, he had managed to pick up a living as best he could, gradually forsaking more ambitious instruments for his barrel-organ, till the tide of life, gradually running low, was reduced to its lowest ebb by the shock of his daughter's death, superadded to the decline which had long been insidiously undermining his system.

"But it will soon be over now, my child," he said; "all the trouble and the nursing. You have been very good to the poor *forestiere* since the *povera* went to the blessed saints. I shall soon see her again, and Anita, and the litle Giulio, in the better country that the *signorina* was reading about; better, she says, than the *patria* itself, with its olives and vines. Ah! I think I see it again, when I dream."

Such a speech as this always melted poor Nelly into tears; and seeing the pain it gave her, he did not often refer to his approaching death. To Lucy, however, he sometimes spoke of his concern for the future lot of his adopted daughter, who was again to be left desolate. Lucy herself had been thinking a good deal about it, and wondering whether she could induce her aunt to take Nelly. Amy, however, arranged the matter unexpectedly. She had been asking Lucy with great earnestness, what poor Nelly would do when the organ-grinder should die; and when Mrs. Brooke next came into the room, she surprised her with the question, "Mamma, may Nelly come and live here when the organ-grinder dies?"

Mrs. Brooke looked bewildered, until Lucy explained the matter. She hesitated, and would have put Amy off with the promise that she "would see about it." But Amy was so anxious to have the point settled, that her mother, at last, gave the absolute promise she asked, and Lucy had the satisfaction of announcing to poor Antonio, the next time she visited him, to his great relief and satisfaction, that Nelly's future home, so long as she desired it, should be with Mrs. Brooke.

XVI.

DARKNESS AND LIGHT.

"Tell me the old, old story,
If you would really be
In any time of trouble
A comforter to me."

FRED came to town for a few days in his Christmas vacation, just as Stella was beginning to recover from the severe attack which had prostrated her. Mr. Brooke's house being so full of sickness, Lucy, though very unwilling to leave Amy, thought it best, on Fred's account, to accept an urgent invitation from the Eastwoods, that they should both spend a week at Oakvale. He would thus have a pleasanter vacation than under the circumstances he could have at his uncle's, where he felt himself in the way, and where

Lucy had so many demands upon her time that she could see but little of a brother whose visits were so rare. The change of scene was very much needed by her, for the confinement and fatigue of her sick-room attendance had had a depressing influence on her health and spirits.

It was certainly, in spite of all her anxiety about Amy, a very enjoyable change to the bright, cheerful, Christian atmosphere of Dr. Eastwood's house, and the bracing influence of the outdoor exercise in which the others made her participate. She felt as if it were wrong to enjoy it so much, when Amy, she knew, was dying, and Stella as yet in so precarious a condition. But God sometimes gives, in very trying circumstances, a buoyancy and cheerfulness of feeling quite independent of the circumstances, which seem specially sent to communicate a strength that will be greatly needed in approaching days of trial; a pleasant "land of Beulah," before the watchers stand quite on the shore of "the dark river." And it can never be right sullenly to close the heart in determined sadness against the cheering influences of God's light, and air, and bright sunshine; nor can we usually, if we would, act so foolishly and ungratefully. That happy week at Oakvale often seemed to Lucy a sort of oasis of sunshine, as compared with the depressing weeks that preceded and followed it.

Oakvale looked scarcely less beautiful, now that the surrounding hills wore their white mantle of snow, contrasting with the intense blue of the winter sky, and the dark green of the pines, while the little river lay, a strip of glittering ice, under the trees, leafless now, which overshadowed its ceaseless ripple in the warm summer days. The young party had pleasant sleigh-rides to see old favorite spots in their winter aspect, and Fred joined the younger children in their skating and snowballing, though he enjoyed much more the walks in which he accompanied his sister and her friend. Mary and he got on as well as Lucy had expected, although she was disappointed that, after their visit was over, she could not draw from him any enthusiastic praise of Miss Eastwood; at which she would have been a little vexed, but for the reflection that Fred, unlike most people, never said the half of what he thought. He did not, however, leave Oakvale without a promise to renew his visit during the summer vacation.

Lucy on her return home, found her little cousin evidently sinking fast. Her strength was almost exhausted, and she suffered a good deal from pain and restlessness; but scarcely a complaint ever escaped her lips. She often talked now about going to Jesus, the thought on which her mind seemed most to dwell. Mrs. Brooke seeing this, at last sent for the minister whose church the family usually attended on Sundays, that being the extent of their connection with it. But he was a stranger to Amy, for his ministerial visits had never been desired or encouraged, and though she was grateful to him for coming to see her and praying beside her bed, she could not speak to him as she could to Lucy, about her willingness to go to the happy home which her Saviour was preparing for her. Still, her visitor could see enough of the change God had wrought in her heart, to

DARKNESS AND LIGHT. 281

make him marvel, as he took his leave, at the wonderful way in which God sometimes raises up to himself a witness in the most worldly homes, and perfects praise "out of the mouth of babes and sucklings."

The little invalid was sometimes slightly delirious when the hectic fever was at its height, but her wandering fancies were always of gentle and pleasant things. She would ask if they did not hear the sweet singing in her room; and when Lucy would ask what was sung, would say, "Jerusalem," meaning "Jerusalem the Golden," her favorite hymn next to the one she loved best of all, "I lay my sins on Jesus."

One night, when she had been asleep for some time, with Lucy only watching beside her, she suddenly awoke, a flash of joy lighting up her face. "Lucy," she murmured faintly; but when Lucy bent over her, she could catch but one word, "Jesus." Lucy saw a change come over her countenance, which she had seen once before, and ere the others, hastily summoned, could be with her, the little form lay lifeless, its immortal tenant having escaped to the heavenly home, whither she had been longing to go.

No one could help being thankful that the sufferings of the patient little invalid were over. Indeed, with the exception of Mrs. Brooke, Lucy and Stella, no one showed any profound grief for the death of a child, who had always been very much secluded, and but little appreciated. But Mrs. Brooke's sorrow was mingled with some self-reproach, that she had not been to her departed child all that a mother should have been, and she suffered now for the wilfulness which, when deprived of one blessing, had turned petulantly from another. Lucy constantly missed her little favorite, and her sorrow for the loss of her father, never quite removed, seemed revived anew by her cousin's death. But she could feel that Amy was infinitely happier in her heavenly home than she could ever have been on earth; and she felt, not only that she should join her there, but, also, that there might be an intercourse and communion of spirit in Christ, incomprehensible to those who look only to things "seen and temporal."

It was Lucy's greatest solace to visit poor Antonio, and speak to him of Amy's concern for him, and her desire that he should find rest and peace in the love of that Saviour in whom she had so fully trusted. He was deeply touched on hearing some of the things she had said, and the tears came to his eyes when he spoke of her kindness in sending so many things for his comfort.

"But," he said with deep feeling, "it was very different for a blessed, innocent child like her, and a sinful man like me." Lucy explained that all are under the condemnation of sin, since none are without it; and that no sins are too great to be taken away by the Lamb of God once offered as a sacrifice for "the sin of the world." He listened silently, while an expression of hope stole over his haggard countenance; and Nelly told Miss Lucy with much pleasure, that after that he prayed much less to the Virgin, and his prayers were, more generally, spontaneous ejaculations, expressing the deeply felt need of a Redeemer.

Stella's grief for her little sister, partly

owing perhaps to her physical weakness, had seemed more violent than that of any one else. The paroxysms of hysterical crying which frequently came on, and an aversion to take necessary nourishment, very much retarded her recovery, and prevented her regaining strength. As the acuteness of her sorrow gradually wore itself out, the unaccustomed feelings of weakness and depression brought on fits of fretfulness, in which all Lucy's forbearance was called for; but she remembered how good-naturedly her cousin had borne with her own fit of nervous irritability, and she generally managed to soothe and pacify her, even when she was most unreasonable, and tired out the patience of both Sophy and Ada.

After the first few weeks had passed, the shadowy hush and solemnity brought by death, gradually passed away, and except for the deep black crape of the dresses, and the abstinence from all gayeties, the family life seemed to have returned to its former tone. So far as external signs went, there was no more realizing sense of that invisible world to which one of their number had gone; no more "looking unto" Him who had been her support in the dark valley, than there had been before. And when a bereavement does not draw the heart nearer to God, there is every reason to fear that it drives it farther from him.

But another heavy sorrow, to one at least of the number, soon followed. One wild, stormy morning in March, when the letters were, as usual, brought in at breakfast-time, Sophy quickly looked up for the welcome letter, with its firm, manly superscription, which regularly appeared twice or thrice a week. There was one with the usual postmark, but in a different handwriting, and addressed, not to her, but to Mr. Brooke. Sophy's misgivings were awakened at once, and on seeing her father's expression as he hurriedly glanced through the letter, she forgot her usual self-control, and exclaimed in agitated tones, "O papa, what is it?" But his only reply was to lead her from the room, signing to his wife to follow.

Sophy did not appear again that day, and the atmosphere of gloom seemed again to descend over the house. Lucy waited long alone, not liking to intrude upon the family distress, till Stella at last returned, still hysterically sobbing.

"They say 'troubles never come singly,'" she said, "and I'm sure it's true. Poor Sophy! Mr. Melville has been killed by the upsetting of his carriage. The horse ran away, and he fell on his head, and never spoke again. Poor Sophy is almost insensible. I don't believe she understands yet what has happened. Oh, what will she do?"

Lucy's heart was repeating the same question. All her sympathies were called forth by so crushing a sorrow, and as she could do nothing else for her cousin, she prayed earnestly that He who could, would bind up the broken heart.

Sophy remained for two days in her own room, and then came down again to join the family circle, evidently trying her best to avoid any outward demonstration of sorrow, though her deadly paleness, and eyes which looked as if they never closed, told how acutely she was suffering. She was not of a nature to encourage or even bear sympathy, and almost resented any instance of special consideration which seemed to spring from pity for her great sorrow.

It was only when shut up in her own room that she gave way to the bursts of agonized feeling which, to some extent, relieved the constant pressure upon her heart. When in the family, she seemed to seek constant employment, not in the light reading in which she had been accustomed to indulge, but in books requiring much more thought, and even some effort to master them. Lucy's class-books were called into requisition, and her drawing was resumed, though she now shrank from touching the disused piano. She had a good deal of artistic talent, and had art ever been placed before her as an ennobling pursuit, she might have attained very considerable excellence in some of its departments. But hitherto she had confined herself to the execution of a few graceful trifles, since her drawing-lessons had been given up on leaving school. Now, however, she seemed to have taken a fresh start, and copied studies and practised touches indefatigably, without speaking or moving for hours.

She would sit, too, for half the morning, apparently absorbed in a book; but Lucy noticed that, while thus seemingly occupied, she would gaze abstractedly at a page for long intervals without seeming to turn a leaf or get a line farther on. Lucy longed to be able to direct the mourner to the "balm in Gilead," whose efficacy she knew by experience; to the kind Physician who can bind up so tenderly the wounds that other healers cannot touch without aggravating. But she dared not utter a word of the sympathies of which her heart was full, and could only pray that a Higher hand might deal with the sufferer.

One wet Sunday evening in April Lucy came down in her waterproof cloak and rubbers, ready to set out for the neighboring church, the one to which she had gone on the first Sunday of her arrival, and which she frequently attended when the weather was unfavorable, or when she had to go alone. She was not sorry when circumstances made this desirable, for she enjoyed the service and the

DARKNESS AND LIGHT.

sermon, more than she did at the church the family usually attended. The words of the preacher seemed to come with more power and tenderness; perhaps, because he had himself been brought, through much tribulation, to know the God of all consolation, and had thus been made able to comfort others "by the comfort wherewith he himself was comforted of God." At all events, it was certain that of the consolation abounding in Christ, he was an earnest and able expounder.

"What! are you going out when it is so very wet?" asked Stella, as her cousin entered the room. Sophy, who had been gazing moodily into the fire, over the book she was holding, started up, saying, "I think I'll go with you, Lucy. Wait a few minutes for me." Her mother remonstrated a little, but Sophy's restless longing for change and action of some kind was often uncontrollable, and the two girls set out through the wind and rain, clinging closely together, to support each other on the wet and slippery pavement.

How earnestly Lucy prayed in silence, as

they traversed the short distance, that the preacher they were going to hear might have a special message to the troubled, heavy heart beside her, and how intensely did she listen to the prayers the minister offered up, to catch any petitions that might seem suited to her cousin's need. She was slightly disappointed when he announced his text, "O Israel, thou hast destroyed thyself, but in me is thy help found," for she had hoped that it would be one of the many beautiful, comforting passages in which the New Testament abounds. But her disappointment wore off as he proceeded with his discourse.

He first briefly sketched the history of the rebellion of Israel in departing from the God of her help, and in transferring to the idols of the heathen the allegiance which was due to the living God. He vividly described the "destruction" which must be the natural result of such a departure from the source of her highest life. Then he spoke of the means by which God sought to bring her back; of the purifying judgments which he sent in love and mercy, to restore her to spiritual health, and of the inexhaustible supply of "help," of tender compassion and restoring power, with which he was ready to meet her on her return.

Having finished this part of his subject, he drew a striking parallel between the ancient Israel and the multitudes of human beings in every age, who, instead of loving and serving the living God with all their soul, are continually setting up for themselves earthly idols of every variety, which fill up his place in their hearts, and exclude him from their thoughts. Wealth, splendor, position, power, fame, pleasure, even man's highest earthly blessing, human love itself, were set up and worshipped, as if they contained for their worshipper the highest end and happiness of his soul. What was the cause of all the broken hearts and blighted lives from which is continually ascending such a wailing symphony of sorrow without hope? What, but the perverse determination of the heart to find repose elsewhere than in its true resting-place; to set up the very blessings which flow from the hand of its God, in the place of the Giver?

Then, in a few touching, earnest words, he

showed how God must often, in mercy to the soul, send severe judgments and afflictions to bring the wanderers back to their "Help;" and of the depths of compassion, of love, of tenderness, of healing, of purest happiness, which were to be found in that divine Helper, who hath said, "Come unto me, all ye that labor and are heavy laden, and I will give you rest."

Never had Lucy heard the speaker more impressive, and she thanked God in her heart her cousin should have been brought to listen to truths which she had probably never before heard with any real understanding of them. Sophy sat back in a corner of the seat, her head resting on her hand, and her face hidden in her thick black veil. She remained almost motionless, until the sermon was concluded, and then they silently left the church, Lucy not daring to speak to her.

Before they reached home, however, Sophy suddenly broke the silence by saying, in a low, agitated voice:

"Lucy, you seem to be what people call a Christian. Can you say, from your own heart and experience, that you believe all that is true about Christ giving such peace and comfort in trouble?"

Lucy replied, earnestly and sincerely, that she could: that she had felt that peace and comfort, when sorrow had been sent her.

"And how does it come? how do you get it?" Sophy asked.

"I don't know any other way, Sophy dear, than by going to Him and believing His own words. They often seem to come straight from Him, as a message of comfort."

Nothing more was said, but from that time Sophy's Bible was often in her hands. Its study, indeed, took the place of her other self-chosen labors, and she read it with an attention and interest it had never awakened before. That she did not study it in vain, seemed evident in her softened, gentler manner, in the more peaceful expression of her countenance, and in the quiet thoughtfulness which she began to show for others. She would sometimes ask Lucy what she thought about a passage of Scripture in which she was interested, and the few words she said about it would give her cousin a clew to the working of her mind. But her habitual reserve had not yet worn off, and Lucy did not venture to trespass upon it.

She expressed a desire to accompany Lucy in some of her visits to the poor Italian, who was perceptibly sinking fast with the advancing spring. He had, however, grown much in trust in his Saviour, and in spiritual knowledge, especially since Lucy had procured for him an Italian Bible, which he could read with much more ease and profit than an English one. He seemed now to have a deep sense of the evil of his past careless life, when even the external forms of religion had been given up, and he had been, like the prodigal, wandering in a far country.

"And how good is the Father in heaven, that he has a welcome home, and a fatted calf for his wanderer," he would say, earnestly, the tears rising to the dark, lustrous eyes, that sparkled so brightly in the pale, sunken face.

Sophy listened, half wonderingly, half wistfully, to the few and broken, but earnest words in which he told of the pardon and peace he had found in "Looking unto Jesus." "I see the blessed words there all the day," he said, pointing to the wall, "and they make me glad."

"Lucy, you have a card like that," said Sophy, as they left the house. "I wish you would give it to me to keep in my room, to remind me of that poor man's words."

Lucy gladly complied with the request, though she missed her card a good deal, and hoped that its motto might be of use to its new owner. Sophy, however, painted the motto in much more elaborate and beautiful workmanship, had it framed and glazed, and hung it up in her cousin's room one day while she was out, with a little slip of paper attached, bearing the inscription, "With Sophy's love and hearty thanks."

One lovely day in May, when all nature seemed rejoicing in the gladness of the approaching summer, Lucy went as usual to visit Antonio, carrying some of the delicacies which Mrs. Brooke still continued to send him, chiefly for Amy's sake. How often might the rich greatly alleviate the sufferings of sickness in poverty, by timely gifts of luxuries which, at such a time, are almost necessaries, yet which the poor cannot buy.

Lucy found the patient unable now to rise, and struggling with the suffocating sensation of oppressed breathing. He could scarcely speak, but he listened with pleasure to the few words she read to him; and as she left him, he pressed her hand convulsively, saying, in a low, expressive tone, "good-by."

Lucy felt she should not see him again in life, and was not surprised when Nelly came next day, crying bitterly, to tell her that her adopted father's weary pilgrimage was ended.

The poor girl remained in the now desolate home only until the simple funeral was over, and then entered Mrs. Brooke's family, where her warm, grateful heart found comfort in doing everything she could for Miss Lucy, whose presence made her new place seem again a home.

XVII.

HOME AGAIN.

"And this was once my home;
 The leaves, light rustling o'er me, whisper close,
The sun but shines on thee where thou dost roam,
 It smiled upon thee here!"

STELLA had been losing instead of gaining strength since the warm weather came on, and her parents were now really alarmed about her, and were considering what would be the best and most bracing place to send her to during the heat of the summer. But Stella, with an invalid's capricious fancy, had formed a plan of her own, and she insisted, with all her old wilfulness, on its being carried out. It was, that Lucy and she should go together to Ashleigh, to stay at Mill-Bank Farm, if Mrs. Ford would consent to receive them as boarders. Her former visit was connected in her mind with pure, healthful, and happy associations, and she thought that the fresh country air, which she so well remembered, and the delicious milk from Mrs. Ford's sleek cows, would do her more good than anything else. It need not be said that the project was a delightful one for Lucy, and as Ashleigh was certainly a healthy place, it was decided that they should go thither under the escort of Fred, who also wished to pay a short visit to his old home. Bessie wrote that her mother would be delighted to receive them, and Stella, with more of her old light-heartedness than she had shown for a long time, hurried the preparations for her journey.

Nelly was to remain in the house, with a kind, trustworthy woman, during the absence of the rest of the family at the seaside. Although she was sorry to lose her dear Miss Lucy, she was much interested in the circumstance that she was going to Ashleigh, and sent many grateful messages to Mrs. Ford and Bessie. To the latter she sent a present of a little silk necktie, bought, with great satisfaction, out of her first wages.

Any one who has ever revisited a dearly loved home can easily imagine Lucy's delight, when from the deck of the steamboat her straining eyes caught the first glimpse of the white houses of Ashleigh and the gray church on the hill; can imagine her delight at recognizing the well-known faces and the familiar objects which, after her long absence, seemed so strangely natural! But the happiness of being once more among scenes so associated with early and happy recollections was not untinged with sadness; for the vividness with which the old life was recalled made the changes seem as vivid also, and stirred up in all its acuteness the sense of loss, which had of late been partially deadened by the exciting changes of her present life. Every step called up her father's image with intense force in scenes so interwoven with her memories of him. It was strange to see the house which had been her home from infancy tenanted by strangers, and to miss all the familiar faces of the home-circle, whom she had almost expected to find there still. It gave her a dreary sense of loneliness, even in the midst of the many kind friends who were eager to welcome back, both for her father's sake and her own, the daughter of their beloved pastor.

Stella's highest spirits seemed to return when she found herself driving rapidly along the road to the farm in the conveyance which Bessie and her eldest brother—whom Lucy would scarcely have recognized—had brought to meet them. Bessie was not much changed. Her good-humored face had more sweetness and earnestness of expression than it had once worn, and her manner at home had the considerate, half-maternal air of an eldest daughter. Mrs. Ford, too, was less bustling, with a quiet repose about her hospitable kindliness that gave a feeling of rest and comfort, and was the result of being less "cumbered about much serving," and more disposed to let her heart dwell on the "better part," on which she now set a truer value. A more perceptible regard for it, indeed, pervaded the whole family, and Bessie and her brother were, both of them, Sunday-school teachers now.

Mrs. Ford and Bessie were much shocked at the change in Stella, whose blooming appearance they well remembered. Lucy had become so accustomed to her cousin's altered looks that she thought her looking rather better than usual, under the influence of the change and excitement. But Mrs. Ford shook her head mournfully over her in private. "She looks to me in a decline," she said to her husband. "I'm afraid she hasn't many years before her in this world!"

But another change, besides the external one, had come over her, so gradually that Lucy had not observed it till now, when the place brought back so vividly the recollection of the gay, flippant Stella of old. She had certainly grown more thoughtful, more quiet, even more serious, and Lucy observed that her former levity had quite departed, and that a flippant remark never now fell from her lips. Her old wilfulness of manner continued to characterize her, but it was owing chiefly to the caprice of disease. She was shy of joining in religious conversation, but seemed to listen with great interest whenever Lucy and Bessie spoke to each other of things connected with the "life hidden with Christ in God." At such times she would look as if she were trying to gain a clew to a mystery which puzzled, and yet intensely interested her.

It was with mingled pleasure and sadness that Lucy once more took her seat in her father's church, and listened to the voice of another from his old pulpit. His successor, Mr. Edwards, though a man of a different stamp, resembled him a good deal in the earnestness of his spirit and the simplicity of his gospel-preaching. The message was the same, though the mode of delivering it was slightly different. He received with kindness and courtesy the daughter of his predecessor, and invited her during her stay to take a share in the teaching of the Sunday-school, an invitation which she willingly accepted, and had the pleasure of finding in her new class a few of her old scholars.

As Stella had a fancy for seeing the Sunday-school, Lucy accepted the invitation given to them both by Mr. Edwards to spend with his family the interval between the morning and evening service. Stella's zeal for seeing the Sunday-school, however, died out with the first Sunday; and after that she always remained with Mrs. Edwards, who, being very delicate, and having a young infant, had been obliged to resign her own class, the one now taken by Lucy. Mrs. Edwards was a sweet, gentle woman, overflowing with Christian love and kindness; and as Stella at once took a great fancy to her, she exercised a very beneficial influence over one who was much more easily swayed by kindness than by any other power.

The celebration of the Lord's Supper was approaching, and as Bessie was looking forward to participating for the first time in the holy ordinance, Lucy gladly embraced the opportunity of making a formal confession of her faith in Christ, and claiming the blessing attached to the ordinance by Him who instituted it. It was pleasant, too, to do so in the very place in which He had first, by the cords of love, drawn her heart to Himself. Solemn as she knew the step to be, she had lived too long on the principle of "looking unto Jesus" not to feel that she had only to look to him still to give her the fitting preparation of heart for receiving the tokens of his broken body and shed blood; and in this happy confidence she came forward to obey his dying command.

Stella had seemed much interested about the approaching communion, and had asked a good many questions respecting it, and as to the nature of the qualification for worthily partaking in it. At last, much to Lucy's surprise, she asked her, with a timidity altogether new to her, whether she thought *she* might come forward also.

It was with difficulty that Lucy could restrain the expression of her surprise at the unexpected question, but she did repress it, and replied:

"It all depends on whether you have made up your mind to take Jesus for your Lord and Saviour, and to follow him, dear Stella!"

"I should like to, if I knew how," she said. "I have been speaking to Mrs. Edwards about it, and she thinks I might come. I know I'm not what I ought to be, and that I've been very careless and wicked; but Mrs. Edwards says if I'm really in earnest, and I think I am,

I may come to the communion, and that I shall be made fit, if I ask to be."

Lucy had not lost her faith in the Hearer and Answerer of prayer, but she had been so long accustomed to regard Stella as one who "cared for none of these things," that she could scarcely believe in the reality of so sudden a change. But it was not so very sudden, and Lucy's own earnestness and simple faith had been one means of bringing it about. Her daily intercourse with her cousin had, in spite of herself, impressed Stella gradually with a conviction of the importance of what she felt to be all-important. And Stella's illness and subsequent weakness, with perhaps a sense of her precarious tenure of life, had combined to make her realize its importance to herself personally, more than she had ever done before. Amy's happy death had made her feel how blessed a thing was that trust in Jesus which could remove all fear of the mysterious change, so awful to those who have their hope only in the visible world. Indeed, she told Lucy that one of her chief reasons for wishing to come to Ashleigh was the vague feeling, derived from her recollections of her former visit, that it would be easier for her to be a Christian in a place so closely associated with her first impressions of living Christianity. And He who never turns away from any who seek Him, had answered her expectations, and sent her a true helper in Mrs. Edwards, whose simple words seemed to come to her with peculiar power; for, from some hidden sympathy of feeling, one person often seems more specially adapted to help us on than another, and Mrs. Edwards had been a special helper to Stella.

Lucy, when she found her cousin so much in earnest, did not dare to advise her on her own responsibility. Stella felt rather afraid of a conversation with Mr. Edwards, but her cousin told her that he was the best person to give her counsel in the matter. Her fear of him soon vanished when the conversation was really entered upon, and she found that she could speak to him much more freely than she had previously thought. He talked with her long and kindly, and finding that she had really a deep sense of sin, and that she desired to come to Christ in humble penitence to have her sins forgiven and her darkness enlightened, he felt that he had no right to discourage her from the ordinance which is specially designed to enlighten and strengthen. At the same time he took care to explain to her most fully the nature of the solemn vows in which she would take upon herself the responsibilities and obligations of a follower of Christ.

It was with a quiet, serious humility, very different from the former mien of the once careless Stella, that she, with Lucy and Bessie, reverently approached the Lord's table, where he graciously meets his people, and gives the blessings suited to their special needs. As they left the church at the close of the service, and Lucy glanced at her cousin, whose delicacy was made more perceptible by the deep black of her dress, she thought that, notwithstanding the loss of bloom and brightness, the expression of serene happiness that now rested on her face gave it a nobler beauty than she had ever seen it wear before.

Before the stay of the cousins at Ashleigh came to an end, Lucy and Bessie had the great pleasure of meeting once more their old teacher, Mrs. Harris, who had come to pay a short visit to her former home. What a pleasant meeting it was, and with what grateful gladness Mrs. Harris found out how well her old scholars had followed out their watchword, may easily be imagined; as well as the interest with which the story of poor Nelly's changeful life and steady faith in the Saviour, of whom Miss Preston had first told her, was narrated and heard.

Lucy did not forget to visit Nelly's stepmother, whose circumstances remained much the same as in former times. She did not seem much gratified by Lucy's praises of Nelly's good conduct. She had always predicted that Nelly would "come to no good," and she did not like to have her opinions in such matters proved fallacious. Lucy, however, rather enjoyed dilating upon Nelly's industry and usefulness, that Mrs. Connor might feel the mistake she had made, even in a worldly point of view, by her heartless conduct.

When the heat of the summer was subsiding into the coolness of September, Lucy and Stella prepared to return home; not, however, without having revisited all the spots which had been the scenes of former excursions, and in particular, the scene of the "strawberry picnic," where every little event of the happy summer afternoon, now so long past, was eagerly recalled.

"And do you remember, Lucy," asked Stella, "how hateful I was about poor Nelly, when we discovered her here? Oh! how wicked and heartless I used to be in those days! And I don't believe I should ever have been any better if you hadn't come to live with us!"

Her physical health had been very much benefited by her sojourn in the country, under the kind, motherly care of Mrs. Ford, who had fed her with cream and new milk till she declared she had grown quite fat. That, however, was only a relative expression. She was still very far from being the plump, blooming Stella of former times.

But the chief benefit she had gained was not to be discerned by the outward eye. It lay deep in her heart—the "pearl of great price" which her wandering spirit had at last sought and found.

XVIII.

A FAREWELL CHAPTER.

"Come near and bless us when we wake,
Ere through the world our way we take,
Till in the ocean of Thy love
We lose ourselves in heaven above."

THOUGH Mr. and Mrs. Brooke marked with much delight the improved appearance of their darling Stella, her medical attendant was far from considering the improvement a radical one, and strongly advised that she should be removed to a warmer climate for the winter. On her account, therefore, as well as on that of Sophy, who very much needed change of scene, it was decided that the family should spend the winter months in the South. Stella was anxious that her cousin should accompany them; but just at this time Lucy received a summons, by no means unwelcome, in another direction, in a letter from Mrs. Steele.

Her aunt had been feeling her strength fail very much during the past year, and expressed a very strong desire that her niece should come to her again, for a time at least. Lucy owed her aunt almost a daughter's affection; and as she had not seen her brother Harry for nearly two years, and as her lessons at school must necessarily be discontinued, it seemed the best arrangement that she should accede to Mrs. Steele's request, and go to the West under the escort which had been proposed for her—that of a friend of Alick who had come eastward for his wife, and was soon to return to his prairie home.

There was some doubt as to what should be done with Nelly during the long absence of all her friends, but an unexpected event which happened previous to Lucy's departure settled that question most satisfactorily. A young market-gardener, who had lately started in business for himself, came to Mr. Brooke's to be paid for vegetables, furnished during the summer. Lucy was sent down to pay him, and was surprised to find Nelly, who had happened to pass through the hall where he was waiting, staring at him in an unaccountable manner, with an excited look in her dark eyes.

"Miss Lucy," she said, in a trembling undertone, seizing Lucy's dress in her eagerness, "wont you please ask him his name?"

Lucy, considerably bewildered, did as she desired, and was startled by the answer, "Richard Connor," and equally so by the joyful exclamation with which Nelly rushed forward: "Oh, it's my own brother Dick!"

It turned out to be really Nelly's long-lost brother. He had followed the rest of his family out to America by the next vessel in which he could procure a passage, but had never been able to discover any trace of them. Getting work for a time as he best could, he had at last entered the service of a market-gardener, where he had done so well as to be able in time to begin business on his own account. He could not have recognized his little sister Nelly in the tall, good-looking girl before him; but time had not changed him so materially as to prevent Nelly's loving heart from recognizing her only relative; and the moment her eye fell upon him, a thrill of almost certain recognition chained her to the spot.

It is unnecessary to dwell upon the delight of both brother and sister at their unexpected reunion, and the torrent of inquiries and replies that followed. Dick had for so long a time given up all hope of finding his kindred that the joy of recovering Nelly overpowered his sorrow at finding that she was the only one who survived to him; and as the young gardener had been intending to live in a small cottage of his own, he was only too glad to claim Nelly as his housekeeper. And before Lucy went away, she had the pleasure of seeing Nelly comfortably installed in a home which she could consider as really her own.

It was no small trial to Lucy, when the time came, to say a long farewell to her aunt and cousins, especially to Sophy, between whom and herself there was now a strong bond of attachment; and to Stella, as to whom she felt a strong foreboding that she should never see her again. Her only comfort was that she could leave the matter in the hands of Him who knew best, and that Stella could safely be trusted to that protecting love which will never leave nor forsake any who humbly seek its true blessing.

With Mary Eastwood, too, it was another hard parting. She spent a day or two at Oakvale before her departure, and both long looked back to that short visit as to a time tinged indeed with sadness, but charged with many sweet and blessed memories.

At last the preparations for the long journey were all made; the packing completed, even to the stowing away of the little gifts from each, and of the large packet of bonbons and cream-candy which Edwin brought in at the last moment for his cousin's regalement during her long journey. Then the cab was at the door before half had been said that they wanted to say, and the long-dreaded good-by was crowded into such a brief space of time that when Lucy found herself on the way to the station, she could scarcely believe that the formidable separation was really over, and that she had finally left her home of nearly two years. She well remembered the winter afternoon of her arrival, and thought with gratitude how many blessings had met her there, and with what different feelings she left it from those with which she arrived there.

The sadness of her departure soon wore off amid the pleasant excitement of the long and interesting journey, made doubly pleasant by the lively and genial companionship of her new friends, who won her heart at once by their warm praises of Alick and Harry; and she began already to look forward to the happiness of their complete reunion as a family—for Fred was to follow her to the West at the close of his theological studies, in the ensuing spring.

When, at last, the somewhat fatiguing but very pleasant journey was at an end, Lucy found Mrs. Steele ready to receive her with a warm, maternal welcome, and Harry, wild with delight, as much grown and improved as they all declared she was. Alick had grown considerably older and graver-looking, under the responsibilities of life and his profession, though he still retained much of his old flow of spirits, and Lucy had the very great pleasure of finding that he had become an earnest Christian man, using his profession to the utmost of his power as a means, not only of doing temporal good, but of advancing his Master's cause.

Lucy soon saw that her household aid was so much needed by her aunt, whose health had become very feeble, that she relinquished the plan she had formed of endeavoring to get employment in teaching during the winter; and between her housekeeping avocations and the claims of Alick's poor patients, whom she often visited on errands of charity, and the carrying on of her own studies, which she was anxious to continue, the winter flew past with incredible rapidity.

When the season of budding leaves and opening blossoms returned, there came tidings, sad indeed, yet by no means unexpected, from the sandy plains of Florida. Stella was dead, but she had died "looking unto Jesus," and in the feeling of her perfect safety and happiness with her Saviour. Lucy could acquiesce in the earthly separation from her. She had seemed to be one over whom "things seen and temporal" held so much power, that perhaps only the pressure of physical disease, and the realization of the possible approach of death could have brought her to the invisible, but ever-present Saviour. Her temporal loss had thus been her great gain; yet still "more blessed are they," who without such pressure "have believed."

Our young friends have now arrived at an age when their history is scarcely so well adapted for the youthful readers of these pages. But as we all like to hear tidings of our friends after years have elapsed, it may be pleasant to catch at least a glimpse of their later life. Lucy never returned to her uncle's house; she became too valuable a member of her cousin's household, to be spared from it; and she is now its mistress in a legal and permanent sense, aiding her husband most efficiently in his labors of love. Fred has, long since, finished his studies and been settled as the minister of a village church near his sister's home. Thither he has lately brought

Mary Eastwood, as the minister's wife, and has found that she admirably fills that important post. The two old friends, united now by closer ties than ever, still delight to maintain their Christian companionship, and to revive, in the frequent visits interchanged, the happy memories of former days.

Nelly still keeps house for her brother, who would not know how to dispense with her multifarious services in weeding his beds, gathering his fruit for market, and tying up his flowers. But, as some of his friends are equally sensible of her good qualities, he has made up his mind that, sooner or later, he will have to let her go.

Ada Brooke has been married for several years, and is much the same, in her present luxurious home, as when we first made her acquaintance, with no more aspiration beyond the transient pleasures of the world. Sophy, who has remained faithful to the memory of her betrothed, is a very angel of mercy, ministering continually to the poor and sick and disconsolate, and finding therein a higher happiness than she ever knew, even in the days when she was most admired and envied. Mr. and Mrs. Brooke, since the death of their darling Stella, have thought more of that unseen world into which she has entered, and less of the present one which formerly so completely engrossed them. And Edwin, finding all earthly sources of pleasure to be but "broken cisterns," has, at last, turned to drink of "the living water, of which if a man drink, he shall never thirst again."

Bessie Ford is still the wise, motherly eldest daughter at Mill-Bank Farm. If, from the uneventful character of her quiet country life, she has not filled so prominent a place in these pages as her classmates, it is not that the watchword, "Looking unto Jesus," has had less influence on her life than on theirs. And though its fruits may have been more obscure, they have been as real, in the thorough Christian kindness and faithfulness, patience, and industry, which make her a much-prized blessing to her family and her friends.

And now, my young reader, that you have seen the effect of taking "Looking unto Jesus" for the watchword of life to some extent illustrated, will you not, henceforward, take it as your own?

If only you come by faith to that Saviour who is waiting to receive you and to renew your sinful heart, and go on living by that faith in him, you will find, ever flowing from him, a life-giving power which will furnish you with the strength that you need more than you now know, for the battle of life before you. And, though you may never be called upon to do things which the world calls great and noble, you will do things in a noble spirit, which is the same thing to Him who looks upon the heart, and

"To make life, death, and the vast for ever,
One grand, sweet song."

www.ingramcontent.com/pod-product-compliance
Lightning Source LLC
Chambersburg PA
CBHW030740230426
43667CB00007B/781